PAOLO FAVOLE

The Story of
MODERN
ARCHITECTURE

PRESTEL
Munich · London · New York

CONTENTS

INTRODUCTION

The beginning of the 20th century witnessed an extraordinary revolution in the historic cultural genres – literature, music and art – bending the rules and traditions of Eclecticism and the conventions of the Floral Movement. Within just a few years many movements sprang up: Cubism, Futurism, Metaphysical Painting, Suprematism and Vorticism, all striving for a new figurative language and means of expressing the true sensitivities of the artists.

Frank Lloyd Wright had emigrated to the United States, where he was building his own, personal, highly successful architectural language, free from any overt external influences. Some architects, now known retrospectively as the 'Protorationalists', were creating their own architectural language in Europe, inspired by engineering techniques, the canons of the Viennese School, Frank Lloyd Wright and the English Arts and Crafts Movement. Their endeavours were cut short by outbreak of the First World War.

In the aftermath of the war, during the brief return to order, other new movements came to the fore, such as Dadaism and Purism in art and Rationalism in architecture. These movements drew on two trends: the Dutch De Stijl (circa 1917) with its abstract shapes, lack of ornamentation and quest for the absolute and the Bauhaus (established 1919), a German school of design and fine arts, encompassing all areas, from architecture to theatre; from furnishings to scenography.

In the Netherlands and Germany some very original Expressionist work was produced; there was also a widespread return to Classicism. The 1925 Paris Exposition launched Art Deco, a kind of geometric, colourful hyper-decoration, which enjoyed great success in Europe and the United States. Supporters of the Modern Movement included some of the greatest European architects: Walter Gropius, Mies van der Rohe, Erich Mendelsohn, Jacobus Oud, Willem Dudok and Adolf Loos, the Russian Constructivists as well as Le Corbusier in particular, given his huge theoretical and practical output and his unstinting activism. These architects disseminated the new canons, taking part in competitions, exhibitions, reviews and international (CIAM) conferences.

The dictatorships in Germany and Russia from the early 1930s put a stop to Constructivist and Bauhaus activities. In Italy however, the Fascist government allowed Academic Monumentalism, together with Rationalism and the Novecento, to continue.

From the 1930s onwards, Scandinavian countries began to make their mark on the European artistic scene, with Alvar Aalto's organic buildings, Gunnar Asplund's Classicism and Arne Jacobsen's Rationalism. Meanwhile, on the other side of the Atlantic Ocean, America was going through a paradigm shift between 1920 and 1940, with some spectacular architectural masterpieces by Wright as well as the advent of skyscrapers, which changed the face of urban architecture. Various architects emigrated to the United States from the Continent, sowing the first seeds of Rationalist architecture in the new world.

Le Corbusier, staircase at Villa Savoye, 1928–1931, Poissy, France
Le Corbusier designed two vertical connections: a long ramp providing an architectural promenade and a spiral staircase, inspired by Constructivist sculpture and Cubist painting.

BETWEEN 1900 AND
THE FIRST WORLD WAR

The early part of the 20th century (up to 1914) was marked by a number of varied architectural trends: the final throes of Eclecticism; Neo-Gothic; Nationalist Romanticism in Northern and Central Europe; organic Art Nouveau in Italy, France and Belgium, with offshoots in Spain, England and the Netherlands; the rigorous Viennese Secession and the folksy, whimsical Catalan Modernism (often included as part of Art Nouveau). Utilitarian steel and glass materials were used in the construction of glasshouses, stations, tunnels etc. This was a lengthy and dispersed period of 19th century revival, with some innovative interpretations, typical of decadent eras. If architecture embodies the physical form of history, it seems clear that the Belle Époque relied heavily on historical prototypes. Despite the evolving times, urbanisation and industrialisation, there was nevertheless a period of cultural stagnation. Against this background, almost imperceptibly, 'revolutionary' avant-garde movements sprang up within just a few years; they were conscious of the zeitgeist as well as African and tribal cultures. These movements were formed by figurative artists, musicians, writers and architects. The first few sparks of Proto-Rationalism, primarily in France, Germany and Austria, were ignited by a handful of talented people such as the pioneers of concrete: Tony Garnier and August Perret, Joseph Hoffmann, Adolf Loos and Walter Gropius as well as the members of the Deutscher Werkbund movement, all of whom rigorously and functionally reinterpreted domestic objects and had a significant influence on architecture.

**Josef Chochol, detail of the
façade of Hodek Apartment Block
1913/14, Prague**

The new figurative vocabularies

A reluctance to abide by historical canons, and a desire to surpass them, led to a figurative revolution in art by members of the avant-garde Cubist, Futurist, Raggismo, Supremacist and Vorticist movements. Two aspects fuelled this ambition: technological progress, movement and speed on one hand, and freedom of artistic expression on the other. Artists felt able to move beyond the two dimensionality of the canvas, to look at figurative and perspectival representation and the immobility of their subjects from a distinctly new angle without necessarily striving for artistic acclaim.

The impetus for change was witnessed primarily in Milan, Paris and Moscow, however due to their eminent notion of modernity, their relationship with progress and industry, their powerful figurative quality and widespread desire for renewal, the movements were to enjoy success internationally. The journey of the devolution from the figurative arts, literature and music to architecture, was hindered by physical and functional factors but nevertheless proved to be significant for the entire mid-war period.

The new figurative language meant that modern architecture rested only on the new canons that declared all historic or floral references to be out-dated and symmetry to be unnecessary. Clear, geometric shapes were sought — squares, cubes and prisms for example — whilst any ornamentation was dispensed with. For architects, the fine artists' search for inspiration from within was translated into a quest for a defining social role, an identification of the needs they had to respond to and the inevitable acceptance of the need to take into account technological and industrial progress.

below
Jacobus Oud, design for houses on the coast, 1917
The architecture is interpreted as a sequence of disjointed, horizontal and vertical freestanding blocks, each pared down to its geometric essence.

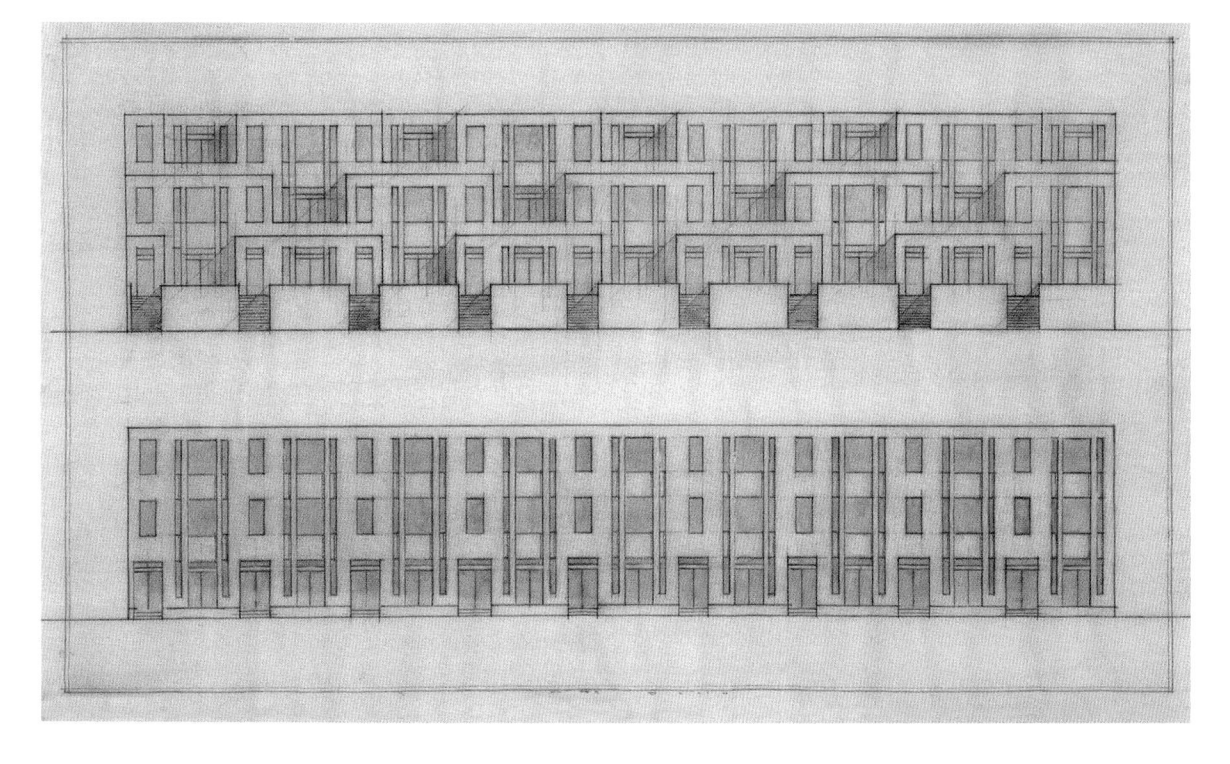

above, left
Pablo Picasso, *Girl with a Mandolin*,
1910
Cubism was an avant-garde figurative
movement in which objects were represented from several different view-
points simultaneously. It also introduced the fourth dimension: time.
Cubism had a direct and formal influence, particularly on Czech architecture, which embraced faceted shapes
and had an indirect effect through
abstraction, Constructivism and De
Stijl. Cubism paved the way for an
architectural style composed of geometric volumes.

above, right
Antonio Sant'Elia, *Electric Power Plant*,
1914
Antonio Sant'Elia (1888–1916) from
Como and Mario Chiattone
(1891–1957) from Ticino, were both
Futurist architects who worked
together briefly in Milan. Neither architect realised their visions, but a great
many architects followed their lead
by designing buildings that bore the
hallmarks of industrial progress, the
production of energy and movement:
factories, stations, silos, power plants,
bridges and multi-storey buildings.
The designs highlight the structure

and the plan layout. Sant'Elia's designs
were innovative and extremely inven-
tive, a world away from contemporary
buildings at that time. Their configuration was extremely dynamic, with each
building representing an aggregation of
volumes and shapes repeated in quick
succession. Movement is represented
by open lift shafts, stairs, funiculars,
trams and trains; whilst technological
evolution is represented by pipes,
chimneys, conduits and tunnels.

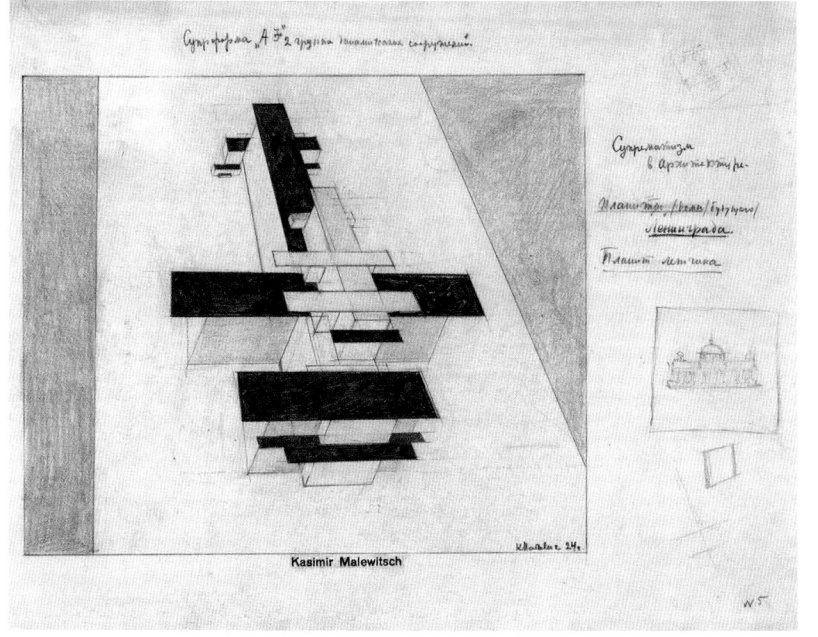

Kasimir Malewitsch

below, left
Kazimir Malevich, Houses of the Future Leningrad: Pilot's House, 1915
Radically abstract artworks such as *Black Square on White Field* (1915) were applied to architectural drawings. The houses are made up of simple, elongated volumes, with scant colour and lack of ornamentation, portrayed in a dynamic, seemingly free-falling sequence, devoid of context or landscape. Malevich applied his volumes to architecture, also influencing the Russian avant-garde movements.

Giorgio de Chirico, *The Agony of Parting*, 1913, (bottom, right) and Giovanni Guerrini, Ernesto Bruno La Padula, Mario Romano (opposite page), Palazzo della Civiltà Italiana, 1938–1943, Rome
Metaphysical art had a direct influence on 20th century architecture because of its volumetric simplicity and geometric reference to classical decoration. It drew on the abstract façades

that formed the streets and squares during the Fascist era. The Universal Expo building, designed to celebrate the twentieth anniversary of Mussolini's March on Rome (1922), was the final and greatest representation of the simplified Neo-Classical style of architecture, which was greatly influenced by metaphysical painting during that twenty-year period.

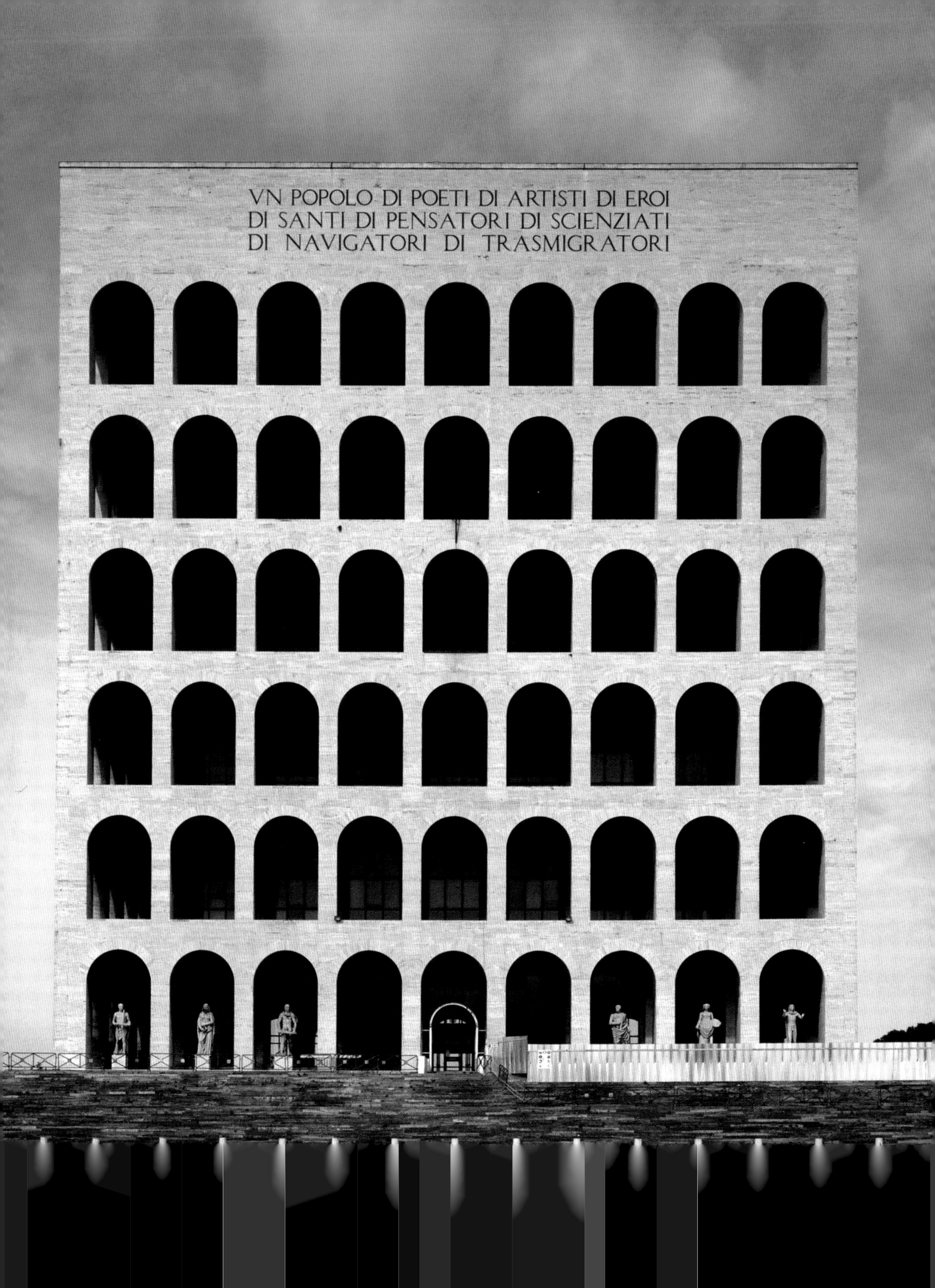
VN POPOLO DI POETI DI ARTISTI DI EROI
DI SANTI DI PENSATORI DI SCIENZIATI
DI NAVIGATORI DI TRASMIGRATORI

CZECH CUBISM IN PRAGUE

Despite its somewhat geographically isolated position, situated on the border of the Austro-Hungarian Empire, Prague had long been a centre of international culture. Cubism and Futurism, the new figurative languages, began to enjoy currency in Prague from around 1910 onwards. As was typical at that time, avant-garde artists split into different stylistic groups.

The Group of Creative Artists was set up in 1911, sparking an architectural style inspired by the most angular and geometric Cubist images. It was a short-lived and unique trend, which made its mark historically.

Villas and residences were built using various different codes — large-scale structures with generous window openings (bow-windows and French mansards) — where elements of urban furnishing were introduced. Their originality lay in the fragmentation of flat surfaces: cornices, gables, columns, window-sills, into faceted volumes, with angular triangular or trapezoidal surfaces resembling folded origami. Furthermore, there was an absence of colour: the idea was to replace naturalistic Art Nouveau decoration with geometric and abstract motifs that served to dematerialise and articulate the façades, so that they appeared to vibrate in a continuous interplay of light and shade. The architects of this movement were locals; none of them were internationally renowned. However, Jan Kotera the 'master' of Bohemian Art Nouveau became part of the group, as well as Brancusi, with his *Endless Column*, which was an elongated reinterpretation of Cubist street lamp designs. The group was fractured by the First World War in 1915, but continued to influence German Expressionist and Art Deco right up to the Paris Exhibition of 1925.

opposite page
Josef Chochol, Hodek Apartment Block, 1913/14, Prague
Hodek Apartment Block is one of the most significant examples of Czech Cubism. It is known for the device of the hexagonal pillar that supports the corner balconies and triangular parapets.

below, left
Emil Kralicek, Matej Blecha, Lamp Post, 1912, Prague
The base/bench and column are interpreted as a repeated, superimposed faceted prism.

below, right
Constantin Brancusi, *Endless Column*, 1918, Târgu Jiu, Romania
Brancusi's most famous work, with its oft-repeated module, is thought to have been inspired by the Prague lamppost pictured below.

PROTORATIONALISM

Some of the many architectural works produced during the five years between 1900 and 1915 can be defined as being Protorationalist in terms of their canons; they are forerunners of the Rationalist movement (1920–1940). These were designed by individual architects, each with their own unique methods of research and expression. Their cultural references were the grandiose architecture and glass structures built by engineers, such as glass houses, urban walkways ('galleries'), railway stations; the *Wiener Werkstätte* (Vienna Workshop, established 1903), the craft studio founded by Josef Hoffmann and Karl Moser, which produced hand-made everyday objects whose only decorative claim was their clear geometric structure — influenced by the *Deutscher Werkbund* movement, which promoted the production of stylistically pared down industrial objects. Further influences were the early works of Frank Lloyd Wright, who was brought to Europe's attention by a portfolio of his lithographs printed in Berlin in 1910. Vienna Secessionist architecture was reacting to an elaborately decorative period with stark stereometric volumes, their corners emphasised by decorations in a form known as 'whiplash' or 'eel'. The Secessionists were also influenced by the work produced by masters from the previous generation.
Peter Behrens, who had made a close study of Neo-Classical buildings, designed a concrete factory building for AEG in Berlin, featuring a steel and glass façade (1909),

Auguste Perret, Garage, Rue Ponthieu, 1905, Paris
While the interior is merely a simple industrial hangar, the façade is a clear glass curtain-wall with a reinforced concrete frame inscribing the large-scale shape of the Renault emblem.

which became a benchmark for young architects. Gropius, van der Rohe and Le Corbusier all worked together with Behrens in 1910.

Josef Hoffmann, a member of the Secession, designed the starkly minimalist Purkersdorf Sanatorium (1903) and later the Maison Stoclet in Brussels (completed in 1914), which was the Movement's masterpiece: a mixture between Secession and Protorationalism. Though few in number, the works produced by Garnier, Perret, Loos and Gropius during this period were essential masterpieces in the history of modern architecture.

World War I broke out in 1914, engulfing almost entire Continental Europe (with the exception of the Netherlands and Switzerland): a catastrophic event of hitherto unknown scale and scope. Many members of the Secessionist group were conscripted to fight and many of them were tragically killed. Their projects were cut short and left in limbo by the onslaught of war: a lengthy and traumatic schism which lasted for years. Works by the Protorationalists, who carried out their own individual research without being dictated to by any particular movement, were publicised by the early architectural journals, later to become reference material for the development of future architects.

Josef Hoffmann, Villa Skywa-Primavesi, 1913–1915, Vienna
Hoffmann's vocabulary consisted of classical elements, such as fluted columns, combined with more traditionally popular elements such as mansards, to produce strictly symmetrical buildings. Every component is drawn geometrically in heavy lines, like the flutings on the columns and pilasters and the window transoms, to create a very different rational vocabulary from that of the contemporary Art Nouveau style.

DEUTSCHER WERKBUND

By the early 20th century, Prussian Germany was the cultural avant-garde centre of Europe. This was thanks to the activities of different groups of artists, as well as an enlightened industrial class and a widespread philosophical mind-set inspired by the idealist rigour of the philosophers, Immanuel Kant and Friedrich Hegel. Various cultural groups were established to spread the ideals of craftsmanship as well as to disseminate new building techniques. Hermann Muthesius (1861–1927), who had become the German Embassy Attaché in London, where he studied English architecture, founded the Deutscher Werkbund (German League of Craftsmen) in 1907. This movement brought together architects, artists and manufacturers, who aimed to entirely transform the production of architecture and industrial design according to three principles: '*Qualität*' as in the absolute, technical and aesthetic quality; '*Sachlichkeit*' as in the synthesis of functional and economic rationality; and '*Maschinenstil*' as in the manner of industrial production. The upholding of the tradition of William Morris' Arts and Crafts movement was thus upheld and progressed into industrial production with basic designs, which had an aesthetic, ethical and social consciousness. The movement enjoyed enormous success and spread firstly to Austria, then to Switzerland and on to England between 1910 and 1915.

The architects produced various designs for buildings (factories in particular) as well new designs for cars, trains, airplanes, houses as well as office interiors and furnishings. Well-known architects, such as Peter Behrens, were involved in the movement, as well as people like Hans-Ulrich Obrist, painter, graphic artist and former member of the Secession. Hermann Muthesius disseminated the teachings into Prussian schools (thus laying the foundations for the Bauhaus). Wright travelled to Germany in 1910 to publish his writings on his innovative single-family houses, whilst Muthesius published *The English House* in 1911/12, steering modern production towards the widespread trend for private homes.

The Werkbund held one conference in 1914 before being forcibly interrupted by the War.

opposite page, top
Henry van de Velde, Werkbund Theatre, 1914, Cologne, Germany
The theatre was an extremely significant building, (later demolished) with all its component parts exposed: foyer, hall, stage set. Its clarity of proportion meant that it was regarded as a Proto-rationalist work, however there was also an Expressionist plasticity of volumes along with Art Nouveau decorative elements.

below
Plan, 1914, Cologne, Germany
The Cologne Congress bore witness to two opposing trends: van de Velde favoured individualism in design whilst Muthesius favoured impersonal standardisation. These differences, together with the onset of the First World War, signalled the close of the first phase of the Werkbund.

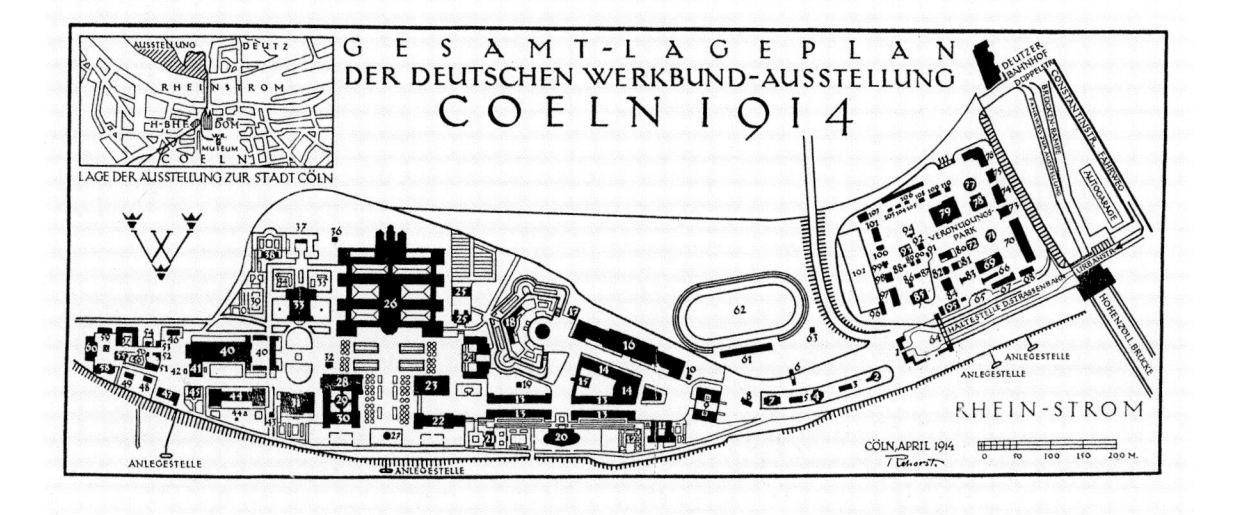

bottom
Bruno Taut, exterior and interior of the glass pavilion at the Werkbund Exhibition, 1914, Cologne, Germany
'Glass architecture' was a deliberately innovative term conceived by writers and philosophers. Bruno Taut designed this centrally-planned building along with its structurally innovative glass cupola, a material that the architect had been studying to test its potential applications.

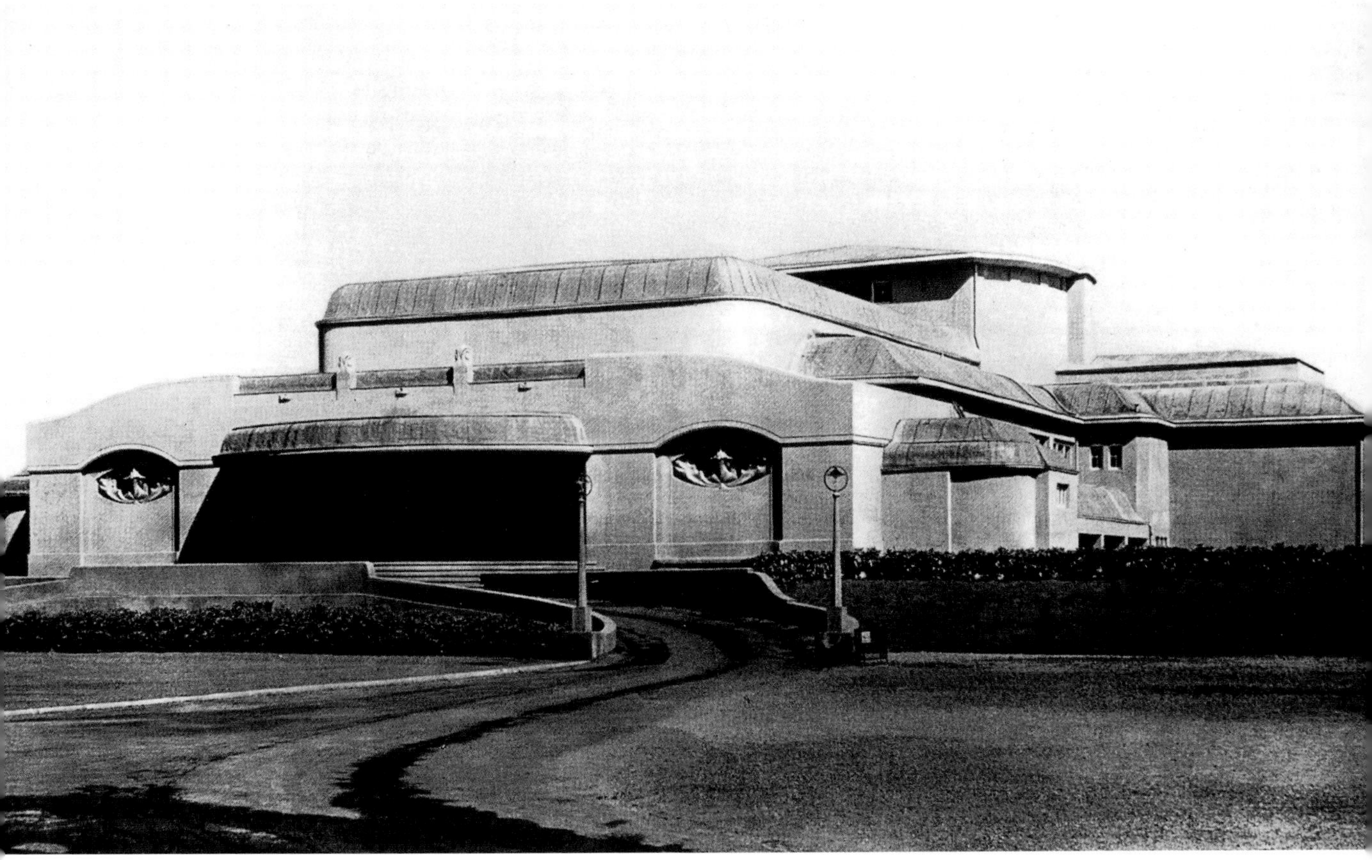

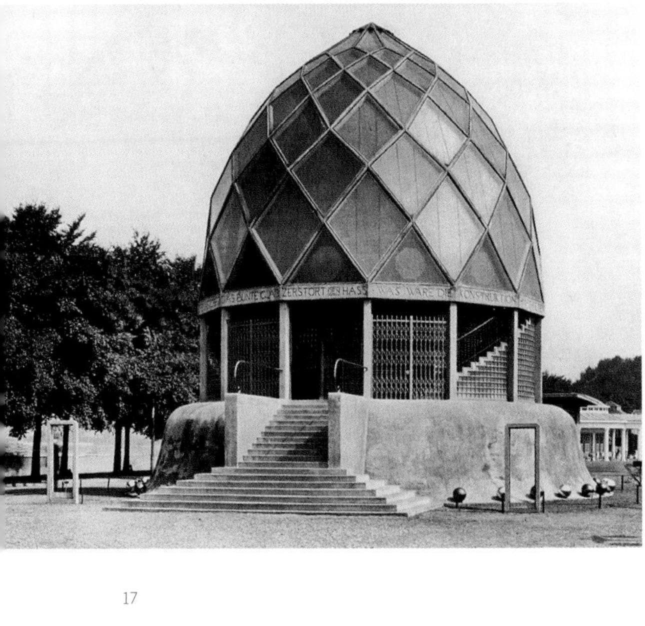

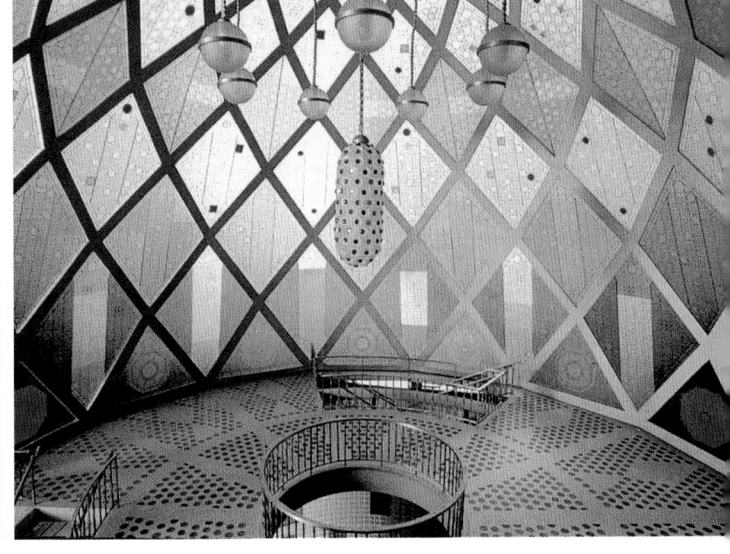

TONY GARNIER

Tony Garnier (1869–1948) was active in two different fields: visionary urban planning and architecture. After completing his studies, Garnier's *Academie de France* prize enabled him to spend time in Rome, where he designed an ideal city for 35,000 inhabitants. He was the only architect of that era to tackle the subject of utopian urban planning. His was an extensive plan, for an 'industrial city' of the future, incorporating the urban prerequisites triggered by the industrial revolution. The plan layout is regular, with parallel streets; the city is located in a fairly flat area between two converging rivers surrounded by hills and served by rail. The design contains innovative elements: open-plan detached houses, pedestrian walkways as distinct from vehicular thoroughfares as well as many trees. The avant-garde design was exhibited without success in Paris in 1904. Garnier then returned to Lyons, but remained distanced from contemporary debate on architecture and no longer wrote theoretically. However, in 1905 the new mayor commissioned Garnier to build several important public works: the abattoir and cattle market (1909–1913), the stadium (1913), the Grange-Blanche Hospital (1915) and the working class, Les États-Unis district. This was an ideal opportunity for Garnier to test some of his ideas for his utopian city with structurally innovative and bold buildings, unprecedentedly Protorationalist in style. The roofs of the houses were flat; there were linear concrete roofs, bow windows and deep cantilevers. The buildings were situated along tree-lined streets.

opposite page, top
Tony Garnier, interior of the Cattle Market, 1909–1913, Lyons, France
Garnier built a pavilion eighty metres wide with structural bays that were extremely ambitious for steel buildings. The design of the building seems to be unprecedented, but assembled with a clear, rational logic, formulated during the time he was removed from his birth place, Lyons.

opposite page, bottom
Tony Garnier, design for an industrial city, 1904
Garnier designed an imaginary rational city of the future, with factories and workers' homes. It was modelled on his utopian view of the world, with wide, open spaces and tree-lined boulevards.

Tony Garnier, stadium entrance, 1913, Lyons, France
Garnier made some concessions to the representational aspect of the large entrances to the stadium, with large arches and stairways, forerunners of the monumental staircases popular in the 1920s and 1930s. The structure was built from reinforced concrete, highlighting the construction capabilities of the new material. The small decorative elements on the upstands, the design of the floodlights and the geometric corner detail are reminiscent of the work of the Austrian Protorationalists (e.g. Josef Hoffmann).

AUGUSTE PERRET

Auguste Perret (1874–1954) was the son of a stonemason-turned-builder; he rejected formal education and accumulated his architectural skills in building yards. The experience he gathered there was put to good use; he set up a construction company with his two brothers in 1905. He thus developed a solid working knowledge of the qualities of concrete, which he later translated into an aesthetic choice: by revealing the structural elements, he believed the authenticity of a building was revealed. He once remarked succinctly, "Construction is the architect's mother tongue." Perret was an innovative designer, decades ahead of his time with regard to the use of concrete; he was the author of stark architectural works far ahead of those of his contemporaries. Distanced from the Maison de Bois Academy in the Parisian suburbs, he trained numerous young avant-garde architects. Le Corbusier remained indebted to Perret for acquiring work for him during the year 1908/09. The open post-and-beam frame raised the question of embedding: in Le Corbusier's first masterpiece, the house in Rue Franklin in Paris (1903), he used sandstone panels with floral decorations (his only concession to Art Nouveau) while employing innovative glass-tiled panels for the courtyard. The façade of the garage in Rue Ponthieu in Paris (1905, now demolished) consisted of a simple frame covered with large sheets of glass with a logo in the centre featuring the Renault emblem. His design for the Theâtre des Champs Elyséees (1911/12), which he took over from Henry van de Velde, was his most important work of the period. The building was renowned for its large-scale reinforced concrete frame, onto which he applied classical decorative motifs as befitted the nature of the building. He built a great many other houses at the time, in which commercial aims overrode architectural considerations. Perret continued to build extremely rational buildings right up to the 1950s.

Auguste Perret, Theâtre des Champs Elysées, 1911/12, Paris
The theatre was a particularly demanding building project, which demanded all of Perret's technical skills. However, he did make concessions to Classical tradition on the façade, with a modular sequence of decorative concrete motifs.

Auguste Perret, interior of the Church of Nôtre-Dame, 1922/23, Le Raincy, France

Perret, who had been a pre-war pioneer, was also very active during the post-war period, designing a great many houses for his construction company. He also took on the challenge of some demanding projects, such as the church in Le Raincy. His mastery of the use of concrete enabled him to create a masterpiece: a church with slender freestanding columns along a nave with transverse vaults and punctured walls echoing French Gothic tradition.

ADOLF LOOS: THE EARLY YEARS

Adolf Loos (1870–1933) began his career in Vienna at the late age of thirty. He gathered experience from various avenues: Loos' father — from whom he acquired a working knowledge of marble and wood — working as a stonemason; spending a few years in Chicago (1893–1896), where he visited the Expo and became familiar with works by local architects from the most cutting-edge school of architecture in the United States. Loos also worked as a bricklayer, fuelling his desire to become an architect, acquiring the ethical and pragmatic values of the American world which required rigour and a strong work ethic to gain professional skills. The work Loos produced between 1899 and 1915 includes several villas, major furniture projects, a large house in Vienna, a department store in Alexandria (Egypt) as well as numerous theoretical works; including a journal (*The Other*, 1902), essays on architecture, fashion and cookery (*Spoken into the Void*, 1900 and *Despite Everything*, 1930). Unfortunately Loos slowly lost his hearing; despite being a shy and an isolated person who was fascinated by myths, his reputation nevertheless grew steadily. There are two main thrusts to his architectural œuvre: on one hand stark exteriors, stylistically sombre and poetic — cubic, white volumes — in other words Protorationalist and on the other hand, sumptuous interiors, overlaid with marble and wood, echoing 19th century Viennese tradition, albeit with geometric volumes. Loos designed Villa Karma overlooking Lake Geneva at Montreux (1906), the Steiner House in Vienna (1910) with its semicircular roof, as well as the Sheu House (1912), which was the first house in Europe to have a roof terrace. His design for Alexandria (1910) consists of a multistorey volume with windows separated by stylised Ionic columns, supporting four floors in the shape of a ziggurat, a solution that he reworked in his post-war designs.

Adolf Loos, exterior of a building on Michaelerplatz, 1910/11, Vienna
Located in the city's historic centre, a tall marble plinth supports a stark, undecorated façade. The building attracted a great deal of criticism at the time, but Loos rose vigorously to its defence, maintaining that it was an excellent example of the integration of a new style of architecture. The precious materials on the façade — the marble columns and plinth — were a prelude to the sumptuous interior spaces (now partially demolished).

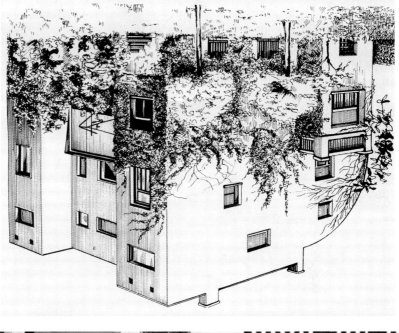

Adolf Loos, view (top) and drawing (left) of the Steiner House, 1910, Vienna

Loos designed the house for the painter, Lilly Steiner. The first-floor studio has large windows overlooking the garden. Loos designed the house to correspond to the height of the neighbouring houses in the street with a semicircular metal-clad roof.

WALTER GROPIUS: THE EARLY YEARS

Walter Gropius (1883–1969), the son of a German architect, embarked on his professional career at the relatively young age of twenty-seven, taking up an apprenticeship in Behrens' studio in Berlin and becoming a member of the Werkbund. His early designs included rural farm housing, a few factories and even a rail-carriage. Stylistically, Gropius was completely removed from Eclecticism and Art Nouveau, building a new language of architecture with great steel and glass surfaces hitherto used only in glasshouses and the roofs of city galleries or stations. Thus, Gropius put into practice the architecture studied by other Werkbund members, such as Bruno Taut and Ludwig Mies van der Rohe, with a nod to Antonio Sant'Elia's Futurist works. Major projects during this period include the famous Fagus shoe factory at Alfeld (1911/12), the model factory and office building, the Werkbund Pavilion, for the 1914 Cologne exhibition. Gropius' vocabulary was more suited to industrial buildings, embodying the image of progress, of workmen labouring in large, well-lit environments alongside a culturally progressive entrepreneurial class. German architects produced a great many industrial buildings during the early 20th century that had powerful, massive volumes where New Medievalism and the search for formal expression converged.

Walter Gropius, Model Factory, Werkbund Pavilion, 1914, Cologne, Germany This model factory was comprised of low, linear volumes. The starkly rational design incorporates some of the formal vocabulary — e.g. protruding roofs, side portals — of Frank Lloyd Wright's iron and steel Galerie des Machines in Paris (1889) and Hans Poelzig's tower in Breslavia, but also introduces entirely glazed components, such as the extra-ordinary spiral staircases, which remain models of unparalleled elegance.

GREAT URBAN PLANNING

The huge urban expansion of the late 19th century triggered the development of urban planning, with some notable results. Thomas Jefferson's Land Appropriation Bill of 1776, issued just prior to the colonising expansion of the vast American plains and the urban boom, dictated street layouts along meridians and parallel lines for cities along the state borders. The bill made an indelible, instantly recognisable mark on the urban layouts of many American cities. The most culturally engaged city, (after the 1893 exhibition) was Chicago, which was transformed by a far-reaching, controlled urban growth plan. The population explosion during late 19 century in Amsterdam called for urban expansion beyond the Baroque city walls. The Dutch architect, Hendrik Petrus Berlage, worked on this expansion from 1901 to 1917, creating Amsterdam South. A number of colonial capital cities were also planned between the late 19th and early 20th century. The layouts of New Delhi and Canberra, both British colonial cities, are particularly fascinating. This is due to the sheer size of the interventions, the urban fabric created, as well as the landscape component, which was derived from the layout of English gardens. The new cities echoed the tradition of crescents (curved streets built along a garden) and 'circuses' (circular streets built around squares or gardens) and drew from early research into garden cities. Unlike other capital cities, such as La Plata in Argentina (1992) and Belo Horizonte in Brazil (1885) — which were variations on Washington's grid layout with diagonal streets — settlements such as Australia's capital, Canberra, were built according to a radial layout. These layouts tended to open out from central squares: a circular one to the south containing the parliament and a hexagonal one to the north with radial tree-lined streets forming other circular squares, which in turn became the central nodes of other radial plans.

left
Daniel Burnham, plan of Chicago, 1912
In 1912 Daniel Burnham and Edward Bennett drew up the first urban plans for the controlled growth of Chicago. Their concept provided for essential alterations to the basic layout to be made, for instance: the creation of wide boulevards, a circular ring road on the periphery of the city centre, a series of diagonal streets radiating from the centre which linked urban focal points, such as public buildings and squares. The city centre became distinguished by skyscrapers; the city, by homogenous expansion.

right
Hendrik Petrus Berlage, Amsterdam South, aerial photograph
Berlage worked on a structured street plan layout accentuated by wide perimeter avenues with some variations to the layout in order to create open boulevards and streets that were not necessarily rectilinear. His plan allowed for large housing blocks (100-200 x 50 metres) with perimeter buildings and courtyards or gardens which remodelled the dense, compact blocks of the historic city centre. The plan was executed by several young expressionist architects whose work was highly regarded.

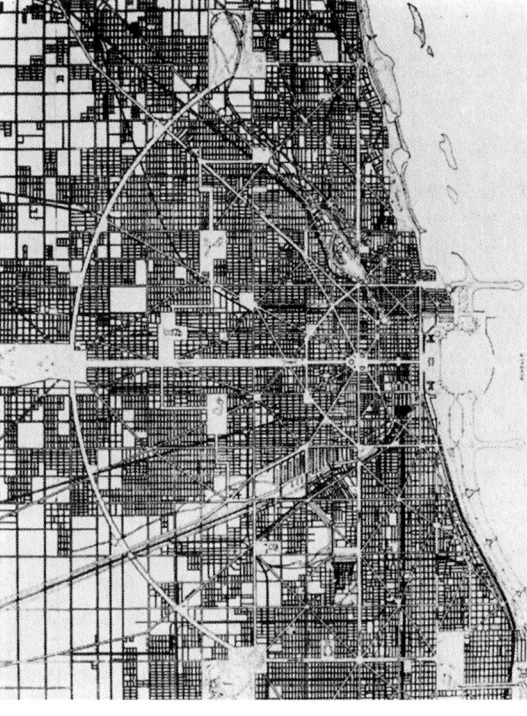

UNITES STATES OF AMERICA

The situation in the United States was entirely different from that in Europe. The Chicago School, regarded as a late 19th century movement, was active between 1900 and 1915. The great number of houses that were built in just a few years consisted largely of single-family housing units or else units for a small number of families. They were largely constructed from timber with a few brick or stone elements. Aerial images of the expansive cities look like suburban villages. Two extraordinary new phenomena emerged: the development of the skyscraper and the significant influence of Frank Lloyd Wright. Skyscrapers were invented in America and were designed according to specific stylistic canons, for instance the combination of the Gothic style with a strong flavour of Eclecticism. Wright was a unique architect: he designed single-family houses modelled on the American lifestyle; his architecture was a cross-pollination between the pioneering spirit of America and the deep-rooted English residential tradition. He developed a personal formal vocabulary inspired by a mix of local aspirations, Japanese domestic architecture and Art Nouveau elements. Wright's designs were so innovative that in 1910, by which time he had made a name for himself, he was invited to travel to Europe for the publication of a monograph in Berlin that was to enjoy widespread distribution and influence. The publication was to inspire the likes of Walter Gropius and Willem Marinus Dudok.

Frank Lloyd Wright, Ward Willits House, 1902, Highland Park, Illinois
Ward Willits House was Wright's first strongly programmatic building. The house has a cruciform layout consisting of four wings extending out towards the four points of the compass from an enormous central hearth; its walls and deep eaves reaching out towards the valley. The house was inspired by the Japanese Pavilion at the 1893 Chicago exhibition which had made a great impression on Wright. The proportioning and rhythm of the windows, the alternating wood and white plaster and the roof morphology bear witness to this. The Australian architect, Walter Burley Griffin, who designed Canberra in 1913, assisted Wright with Ward Willits House.

left
Napoleon Le Brun, detail, Metropolitan Life Insurance Company Tower, 1909, New York
When the Metropolitan Life Insurance Company Tower was built, it was the tallest skyscraper ever built, standing 213 metres high. The tower is built to a square plan; it is streamlined and seems to have been inspired by bell-towers in general and the bell-tower at St Mark's, Venice, in particular. The clock and the loggia reflect this inspiration.

right
Cass Gilbert, Woolworth Building, 1913, New York
The Woolworth Building was the first Gothic-style skyscraper to be erected. Given the great vertical thrust of the building, standing 241 metres high, Gothic architecture was deemed to be the most apposite style of choice; negating the need to resort to the traditional tripartite division of the superimposed Classical orders. The tower diminishes twice along its height

before it reaches the pyramidal roof and the brass lantern at its apex. The terracotta cladding allows for decorative refinements such as small rampant arches, pendants and delicate mouldings

FRANK LLOYD WRIGHT: THE EARLY YEARS

Frank Lloyd Wright seems to have been the architect destined to change the face of American architecture. He was born in the Wisconsin valleys in 1867 and moved to Chicago (the city that hosted the Universal Exposition in 1893) at that time situated on the edge of the frontier. Wright was responsible for designing and developing the sorely needed single-family homes for middle-class Americans. He designed over 200 such houses. Wright was a true pioneer, inspired by the works of writers, Hermann Melville and Walt Whitman. He was self-taught and became the first truly innovative interpreter of an organic style of architecture, where space is generated from within the interior of a building outwards. Wright began his illustrious career with Joseph Lyman Silsbee, an expert in domestic architecture; he then worked with Louis Sullivan, a core member of the Chicago School. He designed single-family 'Prairie Houses' from the late 1800s up to 1915, employing a lexicon of elementary volumes, either plastered white or face-brick, with references to Japanese and Art Nouveau. The plan layouts of the houses were either linear or cruciform with the hearth centrally placed. These were low-slung, houses with generous roofs and deep eaves, their horizontality emphasised by continuous bands of windows and fluid internal spaces.

The non-residential buildings Wright designed during the same period however, were introverted; consisting of stereometric, closed volumes lit from above with angular towers. All the levels of the Larkin Administration Building in Buffalo (1905, now demolished) faced onto a large central courtyard covered with a cupola. The Unitarian Oak Park Temple (1906) consists of two rectilinear volumes which are linked. The church is devoid of ornamentation on the outside but decorated on the inside with protruding volumes, ornamentation and mouldings in geometric patterns; making it a fore-runner of Neo-Plasticism.

opposite page
Frank Lloyd Wright, interior (bottom) and exterior (top) of the Robie House, 1909, Chicago, Illinois
The Robie House is a prime example of Wright's concept for building single-family houses. The hearth is situated at the centre of the building, as was the case in houses built by the American pioneers who migrated, which expanded outwards from the hearth, as in Robie House. The house is low-slung and stretches out horizontally, towards the surrounding valley, which is visible through the continuous bands of glazed windows. The house is surrounded by deep, projecting eaves.

Frank Lloyd Wright, interior of the Humanitarian Church, 1906–1908, Chicago, Illinois
The Unitarian Church, where Wright's father was the pastor, has a decorative architectural interior with piers, balconies and bands with muted colours, serving to emphasise the compactness of the volume, the lack of window apertures and the light that enters the church from above.

WRIGHT: BETWEEN TWO ERAS AND TWO CONTINENTS

Frank Lloyd-Wright's career spanned over so many years and was so varied that it can only be dealt with briefly here. His Prairie Houses period was extremely prolific and full of figurative innovation. An exhibition of Wright's work was held in Berlin in 1910. The exhibition with its catalogue had a tangible influence on the German Expressionists, as well as on Gropius (Werkbund model factory) and van Doesburg. Wright travelled to Italy in 1911 and stayed in Fiesole, just outside Florence. Soon after his return to the United States he was commissioned to design the Imperial Hotel in Tokyo prompting him to travel to Japan in 1915. The hotel (now demolished) was a huge building, comprised of three parallel volumes, where the architect employed a repertoire of previously used forms as well as an excess of decoration. Wright decided to remain in Japan on an almost continuous basis for around five years. He was the first western architect to take the refined principles of Japanese domestic architecture to the United States; his experience in the Far East had a profound influence on him. Wright set up his home in Los Angeles, where he designed several Neo-Mayan style buildings, which had clear references to the palaces at Ixmal and Yucatan. He reformulated geometric volumes in a technique of his own invention, using patterned concrete blocks that imitated the minutely detailed patterns of Mayan ornamentation. The Barnsdall House (1917) and the Ennis House (1923) in Los Angeles were very complex buildings, which also borrow the truncated pyramidal forms from Mexico. Wright's defining project was the compact Millar House in Pasadena (1923), a cubic volume perched above a turret, also known as 'La Miniatura' because of the fine decoration on the tiles. After the completion of this building, Wright remained professionally inactive for almost a decade.

opposite page, top
Frank Lloyd Wright, reconstruction of the Imperial Hotel, 1916–1922, Tokyo
Wright worked in Japan for five years; where he built a school, a station and the opulent Imperial Hotel, where he combined a myriad of decorative styles in order to reflect local culture. The building survived numerous earthquakes; to be demolished and partly rebuilt.

opposite page, bottom
Frank Lloyd Wright, Casa Ennis, 1923, Los Angeles, California
During his time in California, after 1917, Wright fabricated concrete cubes and etched their surface with fine patterns. He used these concrete cubes to clad the walls of some of his houses, in an imitation of Mayan architecture, a stylistic reference blended with other decorative techniques and truncated pyramidal-shaped volumes. Wright used the same ideas in some of his 1950s buildings, as well as in the Californian houses of the period.

Frank Lloyd Wright, façade of the Millard House, known as 'La Miniatura', 1923, Pasadena, California
The Millard House consists of a small orthogonal vertical volume clinging to the sides of a ravine. Once again here, there is a double-height living room, with narrow vertical windows. The walls are constructed with prefabricated blocks deeply etched with a fine geometric pattern.

THE POST-WAR PERIOD

Two very contrasting European architectural movements, Expressionism and Rationalism, were devastated by the destruction of the First World War.

The Expressionists believed that architects were artists, inspired through their subconscious, who sought to create unique buildings using complex plastic shapes that seemed as though they had been crafted by hand. Examples of this architectural freedom of expression are Mendelsohn's Einstein Tower in Potsdam (1922) which looks rather like rocks hewn by wind; or Rudolf Steiner's Goetheanum in Dornach (1928), both buildings like sculptural artefacts made by creative artists. Various works by the Amsterdam School also illustrate this creative spirit.

The artists who belonged to the short-lived group, les Fauves, were more intensely expressive than figurative, as were the artists of the Der Blaue Reiter (The Blue Rider) group, who used spontaneous and intuitive chromatic expression in the depictions of their subjects. Der Blaue Reiter movement existed only in Germany and the Netherlands, in the cultural milieu (myths and fairytales set in suggestive natural environments) from which it had originated. This was an extreme form of creativity that was never really socially accepted by either patrons or the public and which, therefore faded away fairly quickly.

Equally, the cultural platform was being stripped of stylistic, historic and floral nuances, in a search for the new zeitgeist. Le Corbusier and Amédée Ozenfant, the founders of Purism (1918), published the significantly named *After Cubism*. Purism involved the depiction of static, dematerialised objects, in a conscious return to ordered, fluid, plastic shapes that were directly incorporated into the architectural lexicon. Theo van Doesburg in the Netherlands took the concept of order and harmony further still, naming his movement De Stijl (The Style), as in the absolute outcome of formal research, exemplified by Piet Mondrian's abstract and skilfully balanced paintings and Gerrit Rietveld's three-dimensional abstract architecture.

**Walter Gropius, exterior view of the Bauhaus,
1925, Dessau, Germany**

DUTCH EXPRESSIONISM: THE AMSTERDAM SCHOOL

The urban plans that were provided for the large neighbourhoods under the Dutch regulatory plan for Amsterdam South, were built in 1910 by many cooperatives under a special housing law. The schemes were entrusted to a small group of architects who were in their thirties at the time: Michel de Klerk (1884–1923), Piet Kramer (1881–1961) and Johan Melchior van der Mey (1878–1949). All three architects had worked together for Pierre Cuypers (1827–1921), an eclectic architect and pupil of Eugène Viollet le Duc (1814–1879), who was trying to identify a national Dutch style. Cuypers taught his protégés about volumetric proportioning, the use of masonry and the art of detailing. The architects were keen to create their own language, distinct from Art Nouveau and which was unaffected by the latest stylistic vogues such as Neo-Gothic and Neo-Romantic. Their architectural vocabulary was influenced by Hendrik Petrus Berlage's reinterpretation of traditional elements with monumental Neo-Medievalism, their study of the architecture of Frank Lloyd Wright (following the 1910 publication of his monograph in Berlin), their knowledge of the Futurist drawings of Antonio Sant'Elia as well as the volumes of Hermann Muthesius' single-family dwellings. The architects eschewed traditional materials in favour of bricks and ceramic tiles; aesthetically they preferred heavy white-framed windows and imaginative plastic forms. They were less concerned with the typology of houses and rather more with the urban configuration of the housing blocks and the designs of their façades. Particular attention

Piet Kramer, corner façade, De Dageraad, 1920, Amsterdam

opposite page
Michel de Klerk, The Ship, Spaarndammerbuurt Complex, 1917–1921, Amsterdam
A group of young architects developed several new residential neighbourhoods in Amsterdam between 1910 and 1930. They were trying to develop a national style that echoed the Dutch tradition of single-family housing but that also referred to figurative Eclectic, Neo-Medieval principles. Each scheme was large-scale, enabling the architects to create new formal configurations specific to each project, rich with detail and built with great craftsmanship. As was the case throughout the Expressionist period, solving the corners was of particular importance, creating buildings that were precursors to those of van der Rohe.

was paid to solving the corners of the blocks, which were articulated by larger, rounded or protruding blocks. Each project was a new creation: as well as the articulation of the blocks, meticulous care was also taken over the handcrafted detail created by experts from the dockyards.

Between 1915 and 1918 an artist's colony called Park Meerwijk, with large thatched roofs, was built in Bergen (northern Holland). The bulk of their prolific output took place in Amsterdam. Production was not hampered by the First World War thanks to the Netherland's neutrality throughout the War. Following the Berlin design exhibition by Mendelsohn in 1919, links with the new German Expressionist Movement were established. Both movements influenced one another.

NEW VOCABULARIES: DE STIJL

The *De Stijl Review* — a manifesto for Neoplasticism — was initially created by two Dutch artists, Piet Mondrian and Theo van Doesburg, (who was also an author and a writer). The Belgian sculptor, Georges Vantongerloo, and several avant-garde architects, such as Oud and Rietveld, as well as the Italian artist, Severini, became adherents to De Stijl principles. The movement's principles were as follows: the use of elementary geometric shapes for the assembly or the disassembly of shapes; the dispensation of all ornamentation and the use of pure colours. The artists of De Stijl were searching for clear functionality. Their magazine remained in publication until 1928. The movement became hugely influential, especially in Germany; where Gropius published the German translation of Mondrian's *Néoplasticisme (Neue Gestaltung)* in 1925. De Stijl also made its mark on the graphic arts and furniture design, as well as in fine art. Furthermore, the style had a direct influence on architecture: the same formula of painting black lines with white and

**Ludwig Mies van der Rohe,
Brick Country House Project, 1923**
The plan for this project clearly echoed the composition of a Neoplastic painting. This was an approach van der Rohe also used in his acclaimed Barcelona Pavilion (1929). The three, slender exterior wall planes appear to extend into endless space, rather like the lines of Mondrian's paintings.

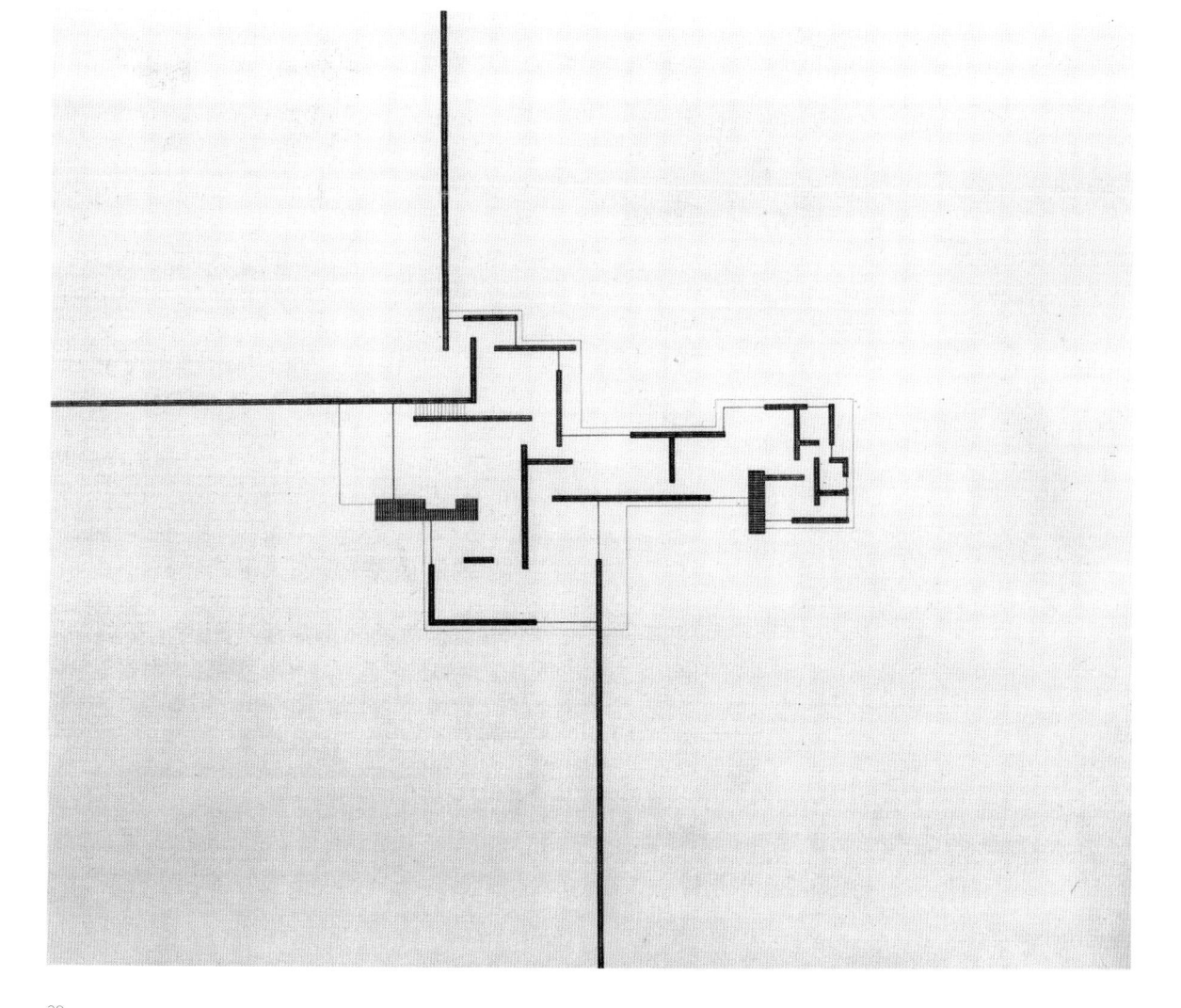

bright red, yellow or blue backgrounds was transformed into three-dimensions as building components along Cartesian axes to create volumes. Each element became a complete volume in its own right, its own physical and chromatic auton-omy being conserved. All elements were kept separate and did not continue beyond the line or point of conversion. The use of curves was avoided as the three orthogonal axes had to continue indefinitely and not end with an arc. The expo-nents of De Stijl never formed a cohesive group: each worked separately on their own work. There were some disagreements over theory, prompting Van Doesburg to leave the movement in 1924. Thereafter, the other artists gradually drifted away, leaving only Mondrian, who remained loyal to the tenants of De Stijl. Mondrian moved to the United States before the War, where he died in 1944.

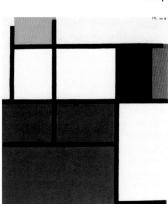

above
Piet Mondrian, *Composition with a Large Blue, Red, Yellow, Black and Grey Bottle*, 1921
Mondrian's compositions are subdi-vided by vertical and horizontal black lines, set in contrast to white or pure coloured backgrounds, to create per-fectly balanced designs with a power-ful impact, comparable to Japanese ideograms or Gothic windows. There is an abstract purity to Neoplasticism where the horizontal plane is modelled with a desire for flat colours (the paint-brush strokes are imperceptible), in a completely flat colour plane. The designs for all his compositions appear as if they could continue endlessly beyond the perimeter of the painting. Mondrian's entire œuvre seems to form part of one single composition, a universal archetype, a platonic idea, which could be skilfully manipulated to create an artwork.

left
Georges Vantongerloo, *Construction within a Sphere*, 1917
Vantongerloo's Post-Cubist sculpture seems to reinterpret Mondrian's work three-dimensionally. His concept sent a direct message to architects with regard to a new way of composing volumes in space.

THE MASTERPIECE
SCHRÖDER HOUSE

Schröder House embodies the compositional theory underpinning the De Stijl movement in general, and Piet Mondrian's paintings specifically. The house was Gerrit Rietveld's first architectural work. Rietveld was a carpenter as was the tradition in his family. He had been a member of the Neoplastic movement (1919) and was driven by a constant desire to experiment; designing and producing furniture constructed with simple geometric rods and panels. He used clear, geometric forms: circles, triangles, rectangles which he assembled or fitted together, in white, black and primary colours, eschewing natural materials in his asymmetrical, dynamic expression of modernity.

This house contains various elements, namely: the measured proportions of the traditional Dutch single-family terraced houses; an arrangement of panels and small volumes that are assembled or fitted together while conserving their own independence; rectilinear, geometric rigour, with the exclusion of diagonals or curves; exterior/interior continuity by means of large windows. Rietveld designed integrated furniture that worked in harmony with his architecture; he had craftsman-like attention to the building as a whole and to the small details, so that his building reads like a piece of beautifully crafted carpentry on a large scale. Schröder House is significant as it embodies De Stijl's architectural manifesto so perfectly that it has remained unique, neither copied nor imitated. Rietveld later embraced the German School of Functionalism, a legacy of Bauhaus. This decision may have been because he believed that he had achieved all he could in this particular genre.

Gerrit Thomas Rietveld, Schröder House, 1924, Utrecht, Netherlands
The façade exemplifies its author's ethos: it is built up of rectangular planes and slender, vertical rods which are arranged in orthogonal layers and which are assembled yet, nevertheless maintain their autonomy. Rietveld accented certain elements with the use of primary colours.

Gerrit Thomas Rietveld, sitting room,
window detail, (bottom, left) and three-
dimensional drawing (bottom, right) of
the Schröder House, 1924, Utrecht,
Netherlands

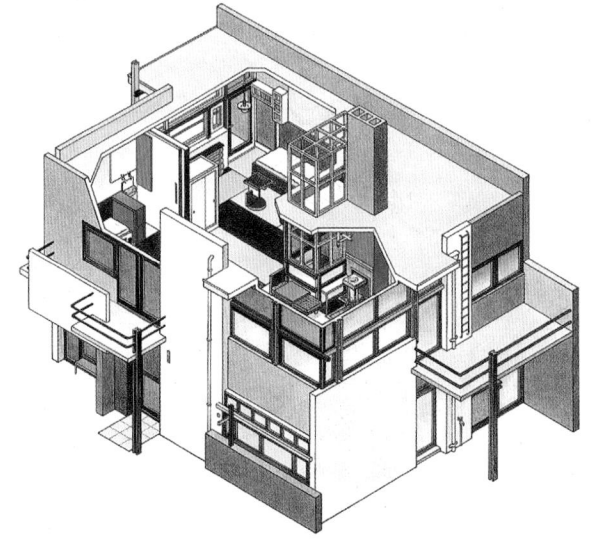

GERMAN EXPRESSIONISM

After Germany's defeat in the First World War, a cross-disciplinary group of artists assembled in Munich. They rejected Cubist shapes in favour of Futurist, industrial architectural dynamics, the figurative deformities of Die Brücke ('The Bridge', a pictorial movement founded by four architects in 1905), as well as Neo-Gothicism and zoomorphism, cross-pollinated with German mythology rooted in nature, mysticism and metaphysical visions. The movement in its entirety was known as Expressionism, but its output was varied and complex. Erich Mendelsohn (1887–1953) drew some extraordinary, highly communicative design sketches during the War. The sketches illustrated large buildings, seemingly sculpted from clay, deeply anchored into the ground. Two such buildings are the pure, white Einstein Tower in Potsdam (1922), built by Mendelsohn himself and Rudolf Steiner's second Goetheanum at Dornach (1928) in off-shutter concrete, moulded like a rock hewn by the wind. Max Berg, Hans Poelzig and Peter Berhren also designed expressionist buildings, factories, water-towers and conference halls, like solid fortresses, their cave-like interiors have over-emphasised visible frames, pendulous protrusions or rippling ceilings.

Erich Mendelsohn, Einstein Tower, 1920, Potsdam, Germany
The Einstein Tower is the best-known and most representative work of German Expressionism. The tower was designed to accommodate scientific experiments into light particles. The exterior of the building is devoid of technical references but is rather modelled like a sculpture, designed to be a freestanding monument dedicated to Expressionism. The building was inspired by one of the many sketches that Mendelsohn drew during the War. It is powerful and evocative. Its shape was innovative and portrayed a completely new concept for an industrial or technical building.

**Fritz Höger, Chilehaus, 1923,
Hamburg, Germany**
This house was one of the Expressionist buildings constructed in the imme-
diate aftermath of the War in Hamburg.
Its vertical and horizontal lines are
fluid; the building is constructed with
dark brickwork and has figurative
detailing at the corner junctions and
on the cornices.

Another group of artists and architects worked on similar forms, yet produced completely contrasting works; some works were totally transparent, there were the myriad of objects designed by Bruno Taut, as well as Mies van der Rohe's glass skyscrapers (1919) built to phytomorphic plans. These were extraordinary precursors of what van der Rohe was to produce post-1945. In northern Germany similar shapes were being used to create traditional Anseatic buildings: the Büttcher-strasse (1920–1931) in Bremen is a small street, lined with masonry buildings that were both traditional and expressionist. Fritz Höger's Chilehaus (1923) in Hamburg reformulated the same shapes three-dimensionally on a grand scale; the superimposition of both horizontal and vertical planes was accentuated at the apex.

BAUHAUS

Immediately after their defeat in the First World War, Germany made a concerted push for recovery in all sectors, thrusting modern architecture to the fore. Walter Gropius was appointed to head up two traditional art schools in 1918. He brought together the two academic institutions as the Bauhaus in Weimar in 1919. Translated, 'Bauhaus' means 'constructed house' or, more accurately, 'planned and built house'. The term 'house' was used as it was a residential school for students and teachers to congregate from all over Germany. The Bauhaus offered courses in aesthetics and design alongside courses on the use of materials and experimentation of their properties in workshops. Members of staff included artists like Paul Klee, Wassily Kandinsky and Mies van der Rohe, as well as other lesser-known highly experienced craftsmen. The concept of the Bauhaus was to reformulate the medieval workshops in response to modern techniques. Gropius believed in the continuity and globality of artistic endeavour; thus there were a wide range of courses on offer: graphics, design, weaving, wood, metal and scenography, to name a few. Gropius was realising William Morris' 19th century dream of integrating the various artistic and crafts activities. Basic courses at the Bauhaus took three years to complete, after which students were able to study specialised courses of varying lengths. Appropriately, the school had close ties with industry when it came to designing everyday objects for mass production. In 1925 the school moved into its new premises in Dessau; three years later, in 1929, Gropius left the school in order to make way for his partner, Hannes Meyer, believing that he had achieved all that he could. This was a laudable gesture on Gropius' part. Van der Rohe took over directorship of the Bauhaus in 1930, but was forced by the Nazis to move the school into a hangar in Berlin. Three years later he was left with no choice but to close the school for good.

The synthesis between innovative, high quality design for everyday objects and industrial production for the wider public was achieved for the first time by the designs developed at the Bauhaus. Avant-garde art movements severed their ties

bottom, left
Lyonel Feininger, front cover for the Bauhaus Manifesto, 1919
The German artist, Lyonel Feininger, painted large urban landscapes; cities filled with housing schemes and gritty urban locations. This image depicts a traditional city set in a different landscape, where celestial stars from the enlightened Bauhaus sparkle.

bottom, right
Albers' workshop, rug, post-1923
The textile workshop run by the husband and wife team, Joseph and Anni Albers, produced numerous abstract geometric rugs. The palette chosen was generally deep colours or simply muted white, grey and black. The surfaces were treated like paintings; influenced by Paul Klee and Wassily Kandinsky. The rugs produced in the Albers workshop are among the best quality works to have come out of the Bauhaus; they helped to fuel the popularity of modern rugs with non-figurative, abstract designs.

with bygone styles and introduced new vocabularies of their own. However, the artists who worked in small groups, remained an avant-garde 'phenomena', appealing to a limited public. Gropius was eager to overcome these limits by responding to popular demand by experimentation and the mass production of some designs. These aspirations underpinned the work produced in the workshops at the Bauhaus. The carpentry department produced furniture with simplified designs; whilst the metal foundry also created some very innovative products. For example, the first chair with a metal tube-frame, which was designed by Marcel Breuer in 1925. Under the Hungarian artist, László Moholy-Nagy, the metalwork department produced a large number of minimalist, highly intricate metal lamps and experimented with light in a variety of ways. The glass workshop under Josef Albers and his wife Anni, created beautiful stained glass windows and colourful, abstract screens. The geometric designs of the woven rugs produced at the Bauhaus were profoundly influenced by paintings of the artists who taught at the school. The palette of browns, reds and ochre shades heralded the advent of modern rugs. Innumerable items were produced for domestic use: ashtrays, coffee pots, cups, in both clear geometric shapes as well as shapes derived from Oskar Schlemmer's theatrical models. In some instances items were industrially produced and were sold at the annual exhibitions held at the school.

Walter Gropius, a staff member's house, 1925/26, Dessau, Germany
Housing for staff members was built in close proximity to the Bauhaus school. Gropius designed a freestanding house for himself; whilst the others were all semi-detached. They were composed of simple volumes in accordance with the Rationalist ethos of the school, but were, however articulated with a great number of balconies on all levels. Bauhaus students designed the finishes for the interiors.

THE MASTERPIECE
THE BAUHAUS BUILDING

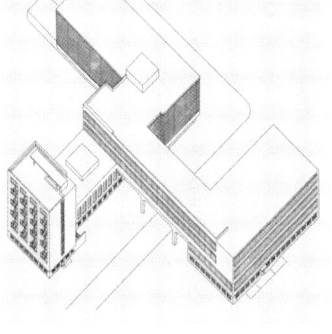

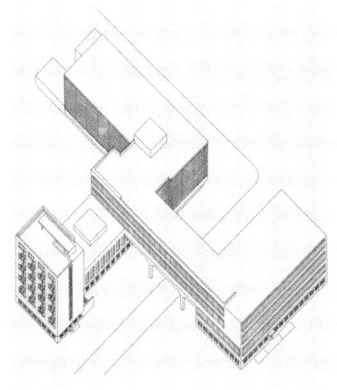

left
Walter Gropius, façade of the students' residence, 1925, Dessau, Germany

right
Walter Gropius, axonometric drawing of the Bauhaus building, 1925, Dessau, Germany

Gropius, in his role as Director of the Bauhaus was, responsible for designing the new headquarters in Dessau (1925). Besides the actual school building, Gropius designed and built several houses for the teaching staff (Paul Klee, Wassily Kandinsky etc...) as well as a dwelling for himself. There were a great many spaces to accommodate: classrooms, workshops, offices, an auditorium and student residences. Gropius' concept was to bring all the spaces together under one roof and connect them by internal corridors in order to create a college rather than a campus.

Each separate discipline of the complex was to be given a distinctive character appropriate to the specific discipline in terms of shape and design. The school was to be conceived rather like a factory — this was an ideological choice — therefore the volumes were to be low and positioned on ground level. The students' residence, however was a multi-storey building; distinctive from the rest of the school. The administrative office block strad-

dled a road — symbolising its role as a link between the various parts of the school. The result was an elongated ensemble of low, volumetrically homogenous blocks, spread out horizontally, creating an unusual footprint.

The form was influenced by the geometric paintings of the Russian Suprematists. The building was designed with two wings bent at ninety degrees that open out like arms, encompassing the outside spaces. Despite its isolated situation, the scheme has a programmatic, urban value. The details were contrived as the blueprint for a manifesto for contemporary architecture. The architecture created typifies the ethos of the Modern Movement: pure white volumes, strip windows or windows positioned in a regular rhythm, small balconies and flat roofs.

The complex has only recently undergone restoration after a long period of decline during the time under during the Communist East German regime.

opposite page
Walter Gropius, balcony detail, students' residence, Bauhaus, 1925, Dessau, Germany
The balconies, placed at regular intervals, were designed as minimalist elements.

LE CORBUSIER: THE EARLY YEARS

Le Corbusier, baptised Charles-Edouard Jeanneret (1887–1965), was born in the small town, La Chaux-de-Fonds, situated in the Swiss Jura on the border with France. His father was a clock designer; his mother a musician. He was educated at a technical school in his hometown that was influenced by the Arts and Crafts Movement. Here he already displayed a precocious talent for inventing and fashioning objects of all kinds. He designed and built four houses while at La Chaux-de-Fonds, but after several trips within Europe, he decided to move to Paris at the age of twenty, in order to realise his dream vocation to the full and to quench his thirst to work and be acknowledged. Paris was the cultural centre of Europe at the time; it was there that Corbusier launched his career as an artist and architect. Paris, like the rest of Europe during the Belle Époque, was undergoing a period of artistic transition, with both the Art Nouveau movement and the spread of radical Eclectic principles. Corbusier's novel approach was at odds with the common practice of using orders and styles from previous epochs to adorn the façades of the city's most representative buildings.

Corbusier met the painter Amédée Ozenfant in 1917, with whom he discussed his theories and set up an artistic movement which he called 'Purism' where objects were defined by their contours alone and were depicted monochromatically: each shape was figuratively reduced, so that its essential form coincided with its physical limits. Jeanneret was prompted to change his name to Le Corbusier in 1920 – in memory of his maternal uncle. He founded the *Esprit Nouveau,* a Rational and anti-Eclectic journal, derived from Purist principles.

His first buildings were single-family dwellings, built according to Purist criteria and Rationalist language. They were white geometric volumes, proportioned according to the golden section; the (almost platonic) a priori materialisation of the conception of architecture as an absolute volume which continues in the interior by means of terraces, small projecting balconies or cantilevered roofs that emphasised the axes of symmetry.

Le Corbusier, design for the La Roche-Jeanneret House, 1924, Paris
This is a semi-detached house, joined by a large, double-volume corner space. This section is completely glazed, with the internal corridors of both houses orientated towards it.

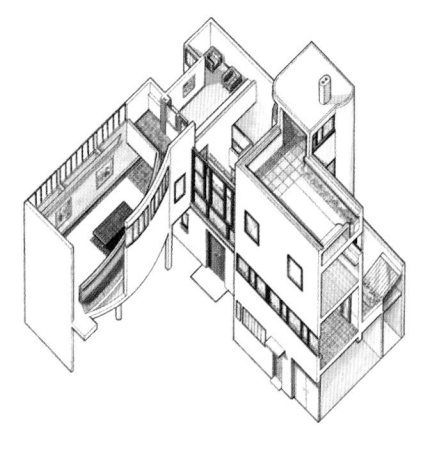

Le Corbusier, Villa Stein, 1927, Garches, France
Besides his theoretical writings, Le Corbusier produced single-family dwellings almost exclusively until 1930. Villa Stein was one of the single-family dwellings built during his early career and demonstrates a continuity of principles. The volume is compact and is plastered and painted in white rising continuously to form balconies. The continuity is only interrupted by pergolas with small, cantilevered roofs.

Examples of this rationalism were the house Corbusier built for Ozenfant in Paris (1922) as two sheds (now demolished) which provided, indirect, homogenous lighting as required by painters, the La Roche-Jeanneret house in Paris for his brother (1924), the Villa Stein at Garches (1927) — with its rigorously proportioned, detailed façades modulated according to the golden ratio — and finally the two Weissenhof show houses in Stuttgart (1927).

In 1926 Le Corbusier and his cousin, Pierre Jeanneret, published *Toward an Architecture:* a Neo-Platonist Illuminist handbook, similar to those produced centuries earlier by the architecture theorists, Vitruvius and Palladio. The volume identified five authoritative and absolute principles for building modern architecture. One of these principles was the 'pilotis' on slender columns, on which the structure was supported. As the building did not appear to be connected to the foundations; a building could be sited anywhere or even copied elsewhere. Roof gardens, corresponding to the building's footprint, were utilised in a practical function such as terraces, solariums, gardens etc. Open-plan layouts, where supporting walls were dispensed with in favour of concrete piers, were liberated from structural constraints; horizontal strip windows blurred the boundaries between the interior and the exterior and provided maximum illumination; finally façades were situated beyond the supporting pillars, thus enabling them to be designed freely without structural constraints.

Le Corbusier, Weissenhof House, 1927, Stuttgart, Germany
Corbusier's experience of building single-family dwellings alongside his theoretical analyses helped him to identify five principles for building new architecture, which he applied here for the first time.
Weissenhof House demonstrates these principles clearly: it is raised above ground on slender pilotis; there is a roof terrace as well as horizontal strip windows, an open-plan layout and façade freed from its structural role. House Weissenhof marked Le Corbusier's first steps towards the design for his renowned Villa Savoye.

THE MASTERPIECE
VILLA SAVOYE

Le Corbusier's five principles of modern architecture have all been applied in this villa in Poissy near Paris, which was built for the Savoye family between 1928 and 1931. If every work of Le Corbusier serves as a kind of manifesto, this building is truly an exemplary one as it brings several ideas together successfully, turning them into design principles. The freestanding building has a square plan; it is sited directly in the centre of an open field, like a small-scale, modern Palladian Rotonda. All four façades are treated the same: plastered and painted in pure, abstract white. The ground floor accommodates only the entrance and the garage, whilst the first floor level contains the living space, almost one third of which is taken up by a terrace. The roof is a solarium, with a screening wall to the north to protect it from shadows. The overall geometric form is offset by the curvilinear forms of the garage, the service stair and the screening wall. The villa constitutes a Purist design in both plan layout and treatment of the elevations. A long, partly enclosed central ramp, connects all the levels to create a kind of architectural promenade; a leisurely journey through the building.

Le Corbusier, corner view of Villa Savoye, 1928–1931, Poissy, France
The spaces open onto a generous terrace contained within the perimeter of the building.

above
Le Corbusier, interior of Villa Savoye,
1928–1931, Poissy, France
A ramp as well as a staircase connects
the floors, to create a kind of architectural promenade from which to experience the entire building.

left
Le Corbusier, terrace of Villa Savoye,
1928–1931, Poissy, France

LE CORBUSIER: TWO URBAN PLANS

Le Corbusier's preoccupation with urban planning was communicated via such extreme schemes that many of them never came to fruition. These were not regulatory plans, but designs for radical urban schemes. The first type of scheme involved the demolition and rebuilding of some parts of the Paris, in order to replace the historic, medium-rise, inhomogeneous urban fabric and its lack of open green spaces with a new urban fabric consisting of extremely tall, high-rise buildings repeated within large open spaces and an orthogonal street plan. The names that were given to the schemes are significant: Contemporary City (La Ville Contemporaine, 1922), to accommodate three million inhabitants, Voisin Plan (Le Plan Voisin, 1925), named after a car manufacturer whom Le Corbusier hoped would sponsor the scheme, in a bid to show that housing, like cars, could be mass-produced, (in this case as cruciform 200-metre-high towers); the Radiant City (1928) which had rows of staggered buildings arranged over an open area.

The underlying principle was that each building should contain thousands of inhabitants that could live there autonomously with their own services (shops, nursery schools, hotels etc.) to create a new image of the modern urbanity as one of identical towers, open streets and generous gardens.

The second type of urban scheme dealt with large-scale solutions which created a powerful visual impact. These were not huge districts, but global visions set in the countryside. Le Corbusier's urban plan for Sao Paolo in Brazil in (1929) provided for two long straight roads, running through the valley, with extremely high viaducts over the hills, culminating in a central group of skyscrapers.

His scheme for Algiers (1931) was even more radical: with a building strip running along a coastal road, large buildings were arranged in a sinuous pattern in the centre of the scheme whilst two other buildings were sited on the promontory. Le Corbusier had designed similar schemes a few years earlier for Rio de Janeiro (1928) and Montevideo (1929) in Brazil.

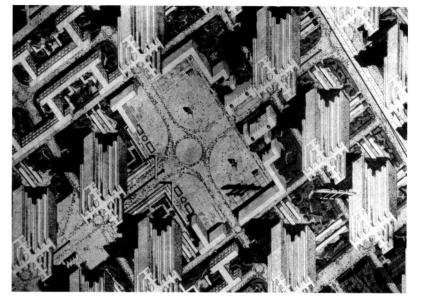

Le Corbusier, design for Le Plan Voisin, 1925, Paris
Le Corbusier had grand ideas about cities: he believed that they ought to be made up of tall, large-scale buildings, like housing blocks, leaving free space for green areas and streets. This urban plan envisaged innovatively formed buildings that he planned and repeated in a novel way.

LUDWIG MIES VAN DER ROHE: THE EARLY YEARS

The ability to rationalise the art of design was one of Ludwig Mies van der Rohe's (1886–1969) great qualities. He learnt to appreciate the properties of materials while training with his father, who was a stonemason in Aachen, and later with a furniture designer in Berlin (1905–1907). Van der Rohe worked for Peter Behrens between 1908 and 1911, during which time he oversaw the work on the German Embassy in St Petersburg. During this period, the architect was powerfully influenced by the Neo-Classical approach of Karl Friedrich Schinkel (1781–1841), which is evident in his first furniture commission, the project for a house belonging to the collector, Kröller, in the Hague (1912), as well as the competition for the Bismarck Monument.

On his return from the First World War, van der Rohe became involved in avant-garde movements along with the revolutionary November Group artists. Furthermore, he was also involved in the *G (Gestaltung)* journal review, eventually advancing to become the vice president of the Deutscher Werkbund. Van der Rohe's first projects were two extraordinary sculptural, transparent steel and glass skyscrapers which responded to the tenants of *Glasarchitektur*. The architect was well informed about the figurative movements he followed. Van der Rohe's facebrick buildings, such as the monument to the founders of the German Communist Movement (1926) and the Krefelt villas (1928) can be described as being Cubist. His concrete country house, with its pinwheel plan layout, was a forerunner of Gropius' plan for the Bauhaus.

Van der Rohe's scheme for a masonry villa (1923) and his masterful design for the German Pavilion at the Barcelona Exposition (1929) are both drawn directly from Neo-Plasticism. Their plan layouts replicate Mondrian's abstract paintings, which van der Rohe knew well. Subsequently, he built the Villa Tugendhat at Brno in 1930, which was a wedding present from the Tugendhat family to their daughter. In 1927, van der Rohe organised the Werkbund exhibition which was dedicated to the house in Stuttgart. He was also Director of the Bauhaus until 1993, when he was forced to close it down in the face of Nazi opposition.

Ludwig Mies van der Rohe, exterior of a glass skyscraper, 1921
Skyscrapers were very rare in Europe in the 1920s. Van der Rohe stripped the building right down to its structural frame, columns, concrete slabs and glass sheets. The skyscraper was inspired by his research into the properties of glass which he carried out in Germany. This research culminated in the 1927 Stuttgart exhibition. Van der Rohe's ambition was to create walls that could be independent of the structure, in order to allow for his demonstrably phytomorphic layout. This was the precursor to the skyscrapers van der Rohe was to build in the United States after 1955.

Ludwig Mies van der Rohe, Villa Tugendhat, 1930, Brno, Czech Republic
Villa Tugendhat was built into the hillside on which it stood; it is entered from above via a glass atrium. The large living room is supported by a network of slender, stainless steel columns with a single, circular ebony screen-wall separating the living area from the dining area. The window has an opening mechanism that enables the entire level to become a large terrace which overlooks the garden and Brno city beyond. The high plinth raises the building off the ground and is reminiscent of Schinkel's designs and Neo-Classicism, as is the case in many of van der Rohe's buildings.

THE MASTERPIECE
BARCELONA PAVILION

The German pavilion at the Barcelona Exposition (1929) was not designed for a specific theme: the building was an exhibit in its own right, a manifesto of the heights to which architecture had risen in Germany. Van der Rohe was given free reign to explore his architectural principles and to showcase German talent. He designed a high podest (the Greek and Roman, and later Neo-Classical crepidoma) which supported the superstructure of the building. He situated the stairway to the side thereby creating a diagonal entrance, along Classical Greek lines. The elevated platform provides an elevated view; whilst the concrete slab is supported by a network of steel columns liberating the walls from their load-bearing function and allowing them to be freely positioned. The plan layout of the walls resembles a Mondrian painting; where independent lines are arranged in a geometric pattern. There are two dark-coloured pools of water: the outer one reflects the architecture like a mirror whilst the internal pool creates a boundary against the perimeter wall, thus abstracting it. Precious materials, like travertine, onyx, ophite, chrome-steel and glass replace the Neo-Plastic use of plaster and primary colours. Van der Rohe also designed black leather and chrome stools and armchairs (the timeless Barcelona Series) for the interiors, which are still in production to this day. Although the pavilion was dismantled immediately after the expo and even though it was only seen by a relatively small number of people, it nevertheless became extremely famous. It was thus rebuilt in the 1980s and remains an attraction to which architects still travel, from far and wide, to admire.

below
Ludwig Mies van der Rohe, entrance to the German Pavilion with the external pool, 1929, Barcelona, Spain

opposite page, top
Mies van der Rohe, interior of the German Pavilion, 1929, Barcelona, Spain
The central space is defined by various glazed wall planes, opaque glass and precious onyx, a travertine floor and delicate silver-chrome steel, cross-formed columns.

opposite page, bottom
Mies van der Rohe, view of the pool, German Pavilion, 1929, Barcelona, Spain
The far end of the pavilion is held by a wall of green ophite. Alongside the green plane is a pool of water which emphasises the wall and furthers abstracts it.

THE WEISSENHOF

The architects of the Modern Movement believed they had a responsibility towards social and cultural change. Moreover, they were unwilling to remain an obscure, minority avant-garde group that remained on the fringe of the main stream. They were very active creating international networks, wrestling with major issues that CIAM (International Congresses of Modern Architecture) discussed, drawing up manifestos and extending their activities throughout Western Europe with dedication, commitment and involvement, unrivalled in the history of architecture. The architects took part in the major architectural competitions in an attempt to spread their ideas, they also published journals and organised exhibitions.

In 1927, the town council of Stuttgart invited the Deutscher Werkbund to build a housing estate. The scheme was project managed by Mies van der Rohe, who invited sixteen renowned architects to design twenty-one dwellings on a terraced site. Jacobus Johannes Pieter Oud and Mart Stam, both Dutch, designed a series of minimalist houses, Le Corbusier built two different dwellings, applying his five principles to both; Hans Scharoun designed a villa with an external Expressionist stairwell; Mies built an apartment block. Peter Behrens, Bruno and Max Taut and Walter Gropius also took part designing housing schemes; Adolf Loos and Gerrit Rietveld were, however not invited to submit designs.

Despite the individual variations, the principles remained the same: rational dwellings, some of them minimalist, simple volumes devoid of ornamentation and flat roofs. This was the 'white district' the Weissenhof, a housing estate that became a benchmark for administrators, architects and critics which remains significant to this day. The experiment was repeated twice: in Vienna (1932) and again, after the War, in Berlin (1957).

opposite page, top
Mies van der Rohe, apartment block, Weissenhof, 1927, Stuttgart, Germany
This apartment block was the largest building in the Weissenhof scheme. The block had four stairways with two apartments per stairwell. The block was only four storeys high without a lift. The building is symmetrical; a geometrically simple block with large glazed apertures. In contrast to the rest of Mies's œuvre, the block represents the moment when he declared his allegiance to the movement with regard to social housing.

opposite page, bottom
Hans Scharoun, Weissenhof, 1927, Stuttgart, Germany
Scharoun, who was less well known than the other architects that have been referred to, developed a volumetrically complex single-family dwelling, with an open, spiral stairway. The architect was inspired by his research into curved surfaces and volumes, which translate Expressionist shapes into elementary forms. Mies situated the building at the front of the estate where the road is curved; mirroring the shape of the house.

Weissenhof Plan, 1927, Stuttgart, Germany
1 Josef Frank
2 Jacobus Johannes Pieter Oud
3 Mart Stam
4 Le Corbusier and Pierre Jeanneret
5 Peter Behrens
6 Richard Döcker
7 Walter Gropius
8 Ludwig Hilberseimer
9 Mies van der Rohe
10 Hans Poelzig
11 Adolf Rading
12 Hans Scharoun
13 Adolf Gustav Schneck
14 Bruno Taut
15 Max Taut
16 Victor Bourgeois

ADOLF LOOS

After the War, Adolf Loos (1870–1933) was appointed to run the Department of Housing in Vienna until 1922. The architect was extremely dedicated to his work during his tenure there. He applied his principles to designs for collective housing, which had roof terraces or small private gardens. These projects were never realised but are nevertheless very interesting, if little-known. Loos took part in a competition to build the offices of the Chicago Tribune in 1922, as he had spent time in Chicago in his youth and as he had greatly admired American culture. His design featured large Doric columns. In the same year Loos designed the Hotel Babylon, which featured two ziggurat structures six storeys high.

Loos had a studio in Paris between 1924 and 1928. He was already well-known there as he had exhibited at the Salon d'Automne. Loos returned to Vienna where he spent his final years working in Austria and the Czech Republic. His output during this latter period consisted of single-family dwellings for various well-known characters, namely: the Dadaist poet, Tristan Tzara in Paris (1926) for Moller in Vienna (1928), Müller in Prague (1930) as well as his house for the Werkbund Exhibition in Vienna. All these buildings are prime examples of Loos' approach with the use of simple white, unadorned volumes. The interiors of the Moller House were sparse, with cantilevered volumes. These were works similar to those being produced by the contemporary Modern Movement; referencing Le Corbusier's early villas. The interior spaces were articulated over several levels, in contrast to the sumptuous pre-war furnishings, they were clad in marble and wood. In 1930, Loos summed up his thirty-year-career by saying that if, at one time, decorated meant 'beautiful' the word was now synonymous with 'out-dated' thus stamping a critical seal on his architecture.

opposite page
Adolf Loos, Tzara House elevation, 1926, Paris
Loos resided for a lengthy period in Paris, where he built a house for Tristan Tzara, the founder of Dadaism. The house has a symmetrical façade with a staircase, pergolas and terraces facing the courtyard. The tall plinth at embankment level is constructed in stone, a material Loos seldom specified.

below
Adolf Loos, Villa Müller interior and exterior, 1930, Prague
The volume of the house is cubic, painted white with symmetrical apertures. The house is broader at the base at its junction with the ground; it also has a roof-terrace enclosed by a pergola that defines the envelope. Villa Müller is an exemplary building of the Modern Movement. As in all his late works, Loos articulated the internal space over several different levels creating a clear composition, with his trademark use of precious materials. The double-volume section is a pure space, while the section of the building on several levels is differentiated by its vertical and horizontal elements.

ERICH MENDELSOHN

Mendelsohn (1887–1953) was a unique figure among the German Modern Movement architects. After the wealth of Expressionist designs he produced during the War, the publication of his work in Berlin and subsequent to the construction of the Einstein Tower, Mendelsohn began an extremely intense period of his professional career, which was also supported by his membership of the Jewish community. This led to a continuous production of fine buildings and new research. He built a hat factory in Berlin (1921–1923) and a textile factory in St Petersburg (1925–1927) with characteristic high, pitched roofs. This morphology inspired Alvar Aalto in his later designs for paper-mills. Mendelsohn was subsequently commissioned to design commercial buildings as well as multi-storey offices, which were a new typology of building at that time. He designed the Schocken Department Stores in Nuremberg and Stuttgart (1926), Chemnitz (1928) as well as the Columbushaus in Berlin (1929). Mendelsohn defined this type of building by employing a structural steel frame behind the façade, composed of alternating planes and continuous windows and curved volumes. Protruding fenestration with projecting horizontal mullions were one of his trademarks. Thus he created an original blend of popular Rationalism and Expressionism.

In 1933 Mendelsohn and Serge Chermayeff won the competition to build the De La Warr seaside entertainment pavilion in Bexhill, England. The pavilion is a white Rationalist building that has a projecting spiral stair enclosed in a curved glass tower with deeply cantilevered external slabs. These elements were devices that remained part of his lexicon and were to be often imitated, even abroad.

With the rise to power of Nazism in 1933, Mendelsohn moved to Palestine, where he built numerous public buildings. In 1941 Mendelsohn moved to the United States where he spent the rest of his life.

bottom, left
Erich Mendelsohn, Schocken Department Store, 1928, Chemnitz, Germany
Schocken department store was one of the many department stores designed by Mendelsohn. The building is illustrative of Mendelsohn's own personal vocabulary, with curved, sculpted façades and alternating opaque planes and plate glass.

bottom, right and opposite page
Erich Mendelsohn and Serge Chermayeff, two views of the De La Warr Pavilion, 1933, Bexhill, United Kingdom
De La Warr Pavilion is the best example of Mendelsohn's purely Rationalist architecture. He and Chermayeff won the competition for this building on the coast, with its extraordinary circular stair tower, designed in Mendelsohn's typical figurative vocabulary. The pavilion is entirely transparent, the cantilevered concrete slabs — visible from the interior thanks to the plate glass — echo the horizontality of the ground plane and the ocean horizon in the distance.

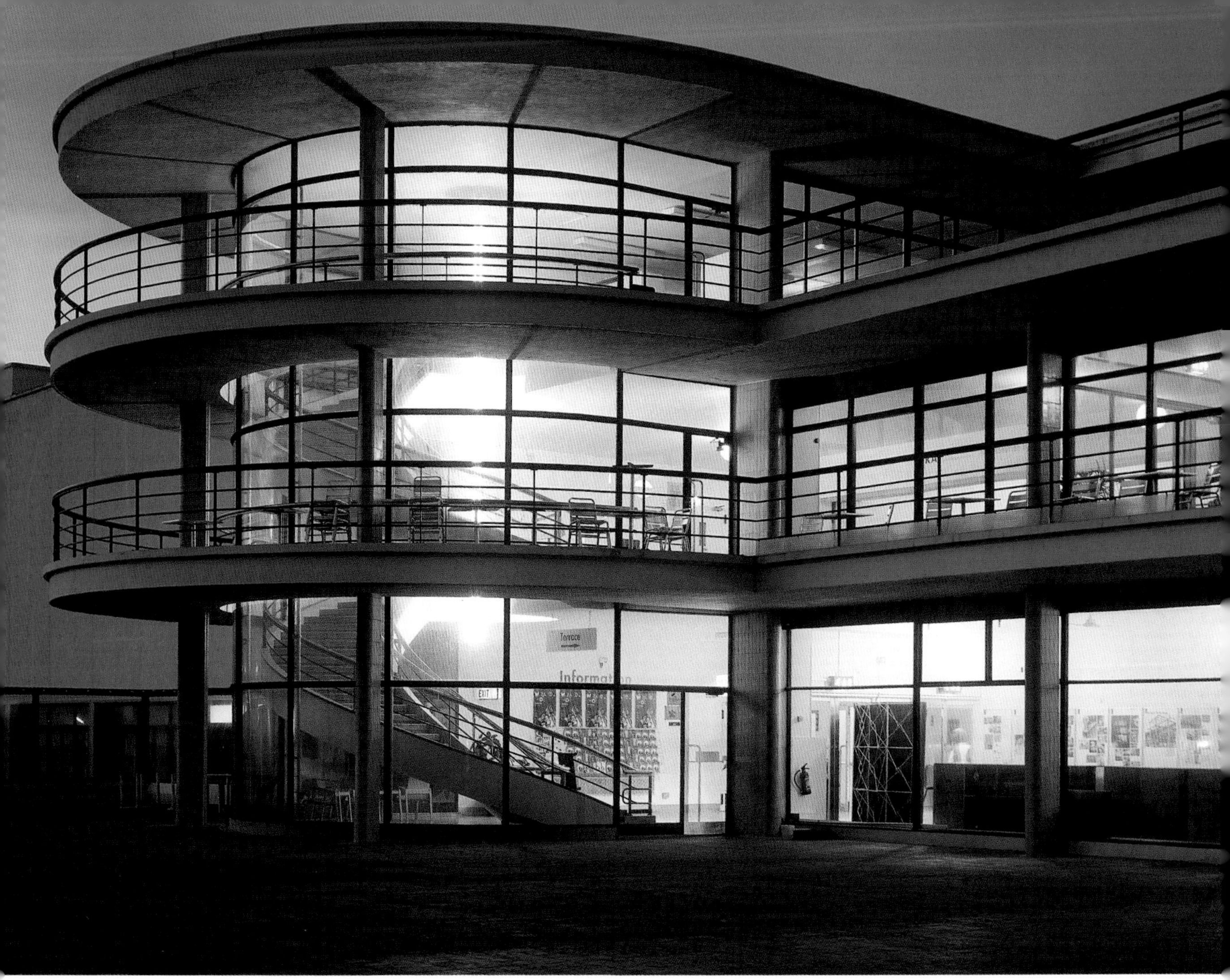
Terrace
EXIT

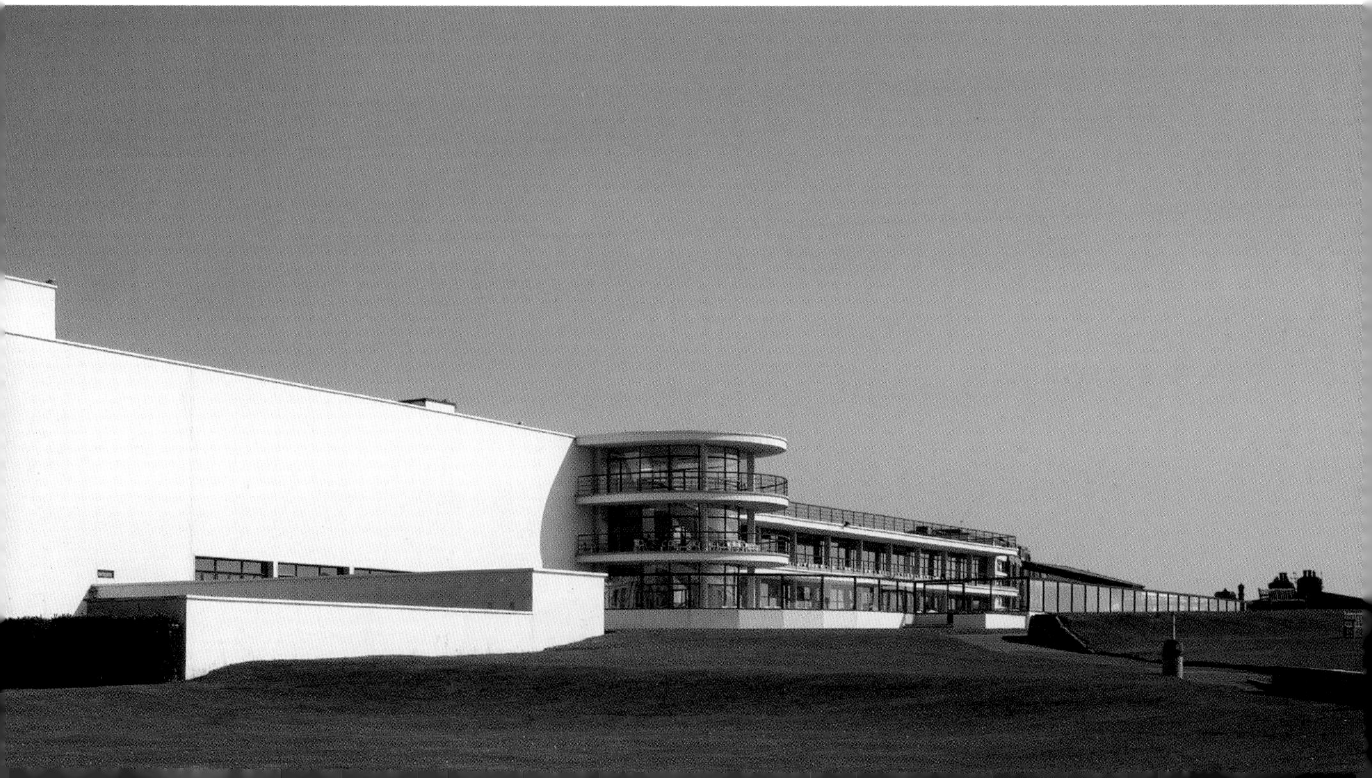

JACOBUS JOHANNES PIETER OUD

Jacobus Johannes Pieter Oud (1890–1963) was appointed head architect to the City of Rotterdam, where he remained until 1933. Oud's work focused on social housing, thus he designed large housing schemes. The volumetric planes of his buildings follow the shape of the site perimeter; they are high density: the Spangen Housing Block (1918) and the Tusschendijken Housing Block (1919) consisted of multi-storey brick buildings with central courtyards with no overt architectural features. Oud's architecture was more influenced by the compact blocks of Hendrik Petrus Berlage — the master of Late Romanticism — than by contemporary Neo-Plasticism.

The architect's next housing scheme, Oud Mathenesse (1922), was situated on a triangular site with four closely packed rows of low houses which, according to local tradition, had monopitch roofs and visually dominant chimneys. Simultaneously, Oud was designing experimental Cubist-inspired projects, focusing his theoretical research on minimalist architecture of abstract purity. He put these ideas into practice in a one-off chef-d'œuvre: two tenement buildings at the Hook of Holland (1924), a town overlooking the English Channel. The blocks were double-storey, white buildings with certain details accentuated in the De Stijl primary colours of yellow, red and blue. The buildings had flat roofs, large windows, as dictated by Rationalist principles and unusual curves. Oud adopted this solution in order to give greater continuity and fluidity to the building mass, which he contrasted with a slender, cantilevered roof that highlighted the horizontality. The cantilevered detail could be defined as being Purist; it was highly praised by critics directly after its conception. The design was used on the cover of a publication on the history of architecture published a few years later in the United States.

opposite page
Jacobus Johannes Pieter Oud, row of houses, 1924, Hook of Holland, Netherlands
The ends of the two elongated, low building blocks have broad, expressive curved surfaces, inspired by Purist forms, bestowing fluidity and continuity to the façades. Oud achieved the formal abstraction that he had sought through his study of avant-garde movements. His design solution soon became internationally renowned.

Jacobus Johannes Pieter Oud, Cafè De Unie façade design 1925, Rotterdam, Netherlands
Oud was one of the founders of the *De Stijl* journal review. The small Cafè De Unie situated in the centre of Rotterdam (subsequently demolished) had a floor plan which is reminiscent of Mondrian's compositions. It was unique in Oud's large œuvre.

In his later scheme for the working-class, Kiefhoek Estate in Rotterdam (1925), Oud designed small double-story duplexes, in acknowledgement of contemporary research into the design of 'existential minimum' housing. The uniformity of design served to bring together the double-storey buildings, with their strip windows and high-quality details.

Oud took part in the Weissenhof project in 1927, designing minimal houses in line with the kind of projects he was involved with at the time. After 1933, Oud freelanced again, designing Neo-Classical public buildings in keeping with the evolving trend in countries with authoritarian regimes. He also designed some houses; reverting to Neo-Plastic designs only late on in his career.

WILLEM MARINUS DUDOK

Several different architectural movements flourished in the Netherlands during the 1920s: the Expressionists in Amsterdam, De Stijl in Utrecht, Oud's Modern Movement in Rotterdam and the individualist, Willem Marinus Dudok (1884–1974) in Hilversum. Like Oud, Dudok was an urban planner. In 1917 he designed the masterplan plan for Hilversum after which he designed and built a large number of public buildings: primarily schools and housing estates, which embodied his vision of a large-scale garden-city suburb. Dudok's design vocabulary developed gradually over time. He was influenced by Hendrik Petrus Berlage's compact masonry blocks and the Late Eclecticism of the latter part of the 19th century, deconstructed along De Stijl lines, in regular prismatic volumes and skilfully reassembled asymmetrically, according to the principles of the Organic Movement. Dudok's elongated, low-rise buildings sat firmly on the ground whilst also possessing an urban eloquence, thanks to the tower. The elements of his designs were strongly influenced by the Larkin Building and Wright's early Prairie Houses. For instance, Dudok used frames that defined the masses, deep cantilevers and white finishes, all formulated with a fine attention to detail. Along his planar façades, he created small accents, as for example in three of the many schools he designed: Minckelers (1925), Fabritius (1926/27) and Valerius schools (1930). One of the schools he designed was situated in the municipality of Hilversum (1921–1924): a building with a central courtyard and a prominent tower at the entrance, preceded by a large pool of water. Architectural critics failed to recognise the quality of Dudok's work immediately; taking some time to acknowledge his talent as an architect and skilled interpreter of the figurative trends of his time which he applied to Dutch tradition in a completely original manner. Dudok produced fewer buildings after the 1930s.

below, left
Willem Marinus Dudok, Bavinck School, 1921/22, Hilversum, Netherlands
Dudok employed elementary geometric blocks put together horizontally and vertically in a balanced fashion, according to various symmetrical axes and successive retreating planes.

below, right and opposite
Willem Marinus Dudok, City Hall, 1921–1924, Hilversum, Netherlands
The Hilversum City Hall is generally considered to be Dudok's masterpiece. This project encompasses the principles of his personal code. Thus, the building has an asymmetrical composition of prismatic masses with dynamically juxtaposed façades arranged like a series of stacked building blocks. This is the result of the deconstruction of the constituent elements, as per the tenants of De Stijl, reassembled according to the criteria of organic architecture. The tower at the corner of the entrance emphasises the building's representative function. The main façade is reflected in a water pool. Every volume is demarcated by the cornices and the planar brick surfaces are articulated at regular intervals. The entrance, with its cantilevered roof, generous windows and white profiles, is the part of the building that most reflects the profound influence that Wright had on Dudok.

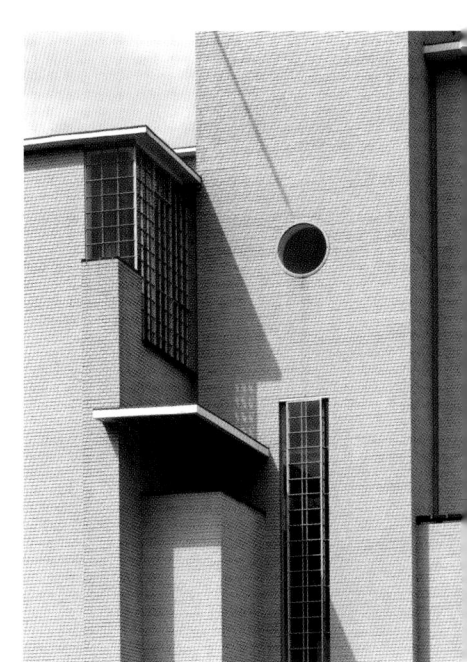

AVANT-GARDE AND DECLINE IN THE SOVIET UNION

The Soviet Union also underwent a process of artistic renewal with Malevich's Supremacist conceptions (1913). The superiority of the artist was affirmed; his freedom of expression was esponsed which led to Constructivism in architecture. In 1914 the Italian architect, Filippo Tommaso Marinetti, travelled to Russia to meet Futurists there; he subsequently kept up his contacts with the Russian Futurists for a decade. Malevich's links with the Bauhaus, (which supported the Russian *SA Review-Modern Architecture* — from 1925 onwards), began to be forged from 1920 onwards. In 1920 the constructivist, Vladimir Tatlin, designed the Monument to the Third International Exposition. His design was an enormous steel structure which rose upwards in a sloping spiral, symbolising the liberation of the people. The tower emulated the Eiffel Tower; aspiring to becoming its Soviet counterpart. In 1924 Aleksej Schusev, a former academic, was commissioned to design Lenin's mausoleum in Moscow. Schusev was inspired by the shape of ziggurats. In contrast, the symbolism of Ilya Golosov, who aimed to build a lexicon of shapes that would have particular psychological effects on their onlookers, was quite different. The Minister of Culture, who had lived in Italy and France for lengthy periods, was also in charge of international relations. He invited Le Corbusier to design the Soyuz (1925–1936) and also to hold conferences in the Soviet Union. In the aftermath of the 1917 October Revolution, young architects were searching for new forms to represent Bolshevik architecture. Form took on free associations; for example the ASNOVA (Association of New Architects), which promoted the need for radically new plastic forms, or the Melnikov's Rusakov Tramworkers Club (1929) in Moscow and the SASS (Section of Architects for Socialist Construction) who favoured pure Rationalism. The SASS, who published the *SA Review,* as well as Moisei Ginzburg, who built the extraordinary Dom Kommuna (1929) in Moscow, were exponents of Rationalism, as were the Vesnin brothers. The WOPRA (Pan-Russian Society of Proletarian Architects) promoted precisely opposing ideas, believing that both the ASNOVA and the SASS deviated ideologically. Its adherents designed monumental public buildings, such as the Palace of the Soviets in Moscow, which is astoundingly high. The architect of the Palace of the

below, left
Konstantin Melnikov, Tramworkers Club façade, 1929, Moscow
Melnikov was an exponent of the ASNOVA (New Modern Architecture) group. He designed expressive buildings, such as this suburban workingmen's club in Moscow. The clubhouse accommodated three meeting rooms with a common atrium. The building exemplifies the fragmentation of forms derived from Cubism and Suprematism, achieved by exploiting the plastic qualities of reinforced concrete to the full.

below, right
Moisei Ginzburg, internal corridor, Dom Kommuna, 1929, Moscow
The design for this building was unusual for its typology. There are two long corridors internally which are rather like enclosed galleries that create access to compact dwelling units arranged over two or three floors. The longitudinal residential wing is connected to the other wing which contains the common rooms: gymnasium, laundry, communal kitchen etc. Various imitations were built on Russian territory, but all are sadly now in disrepair.

Vladimir Tatlin, monument to the Third International, 1920
Tatlin designed a colossal monument to the Socialist Third International, which was a reinterpretation of the Eiffel Tower. A spiral form represented the gradual liberation of the populace.

Soviets, Boris Iofan (1929), was an architect favoured by the regime; he managed to surpass other famous competitors for the project such as Gropius, Mendelsohn and Le Corbusier. In 1932 Stalin decreed that all independent institutions be dissolved and dictated that all works for the regime be monumental Greek, Neo-Classical buildings. Thus the Soviets embraced the Russian traditional religious cultural links with Greece once again through Orthodox Greek Christianity. Thus Soviet architecture turned its back on contemporary trends. Magnificent projects, like the monumental underground stations in Moscow and the sumptuous buildings in Leningrad, sprang up everywhere. Internationally, the vocabulary of the two pavilions at the Paris Exhibition of 1935 and the New York Exhibition of 1937 was monumental Neo-Constructivist. From 1938 onwards, however, in the Soviet Union as in Europe, there was a return to the various vernacular forms traditionally used in regional buildings (Armenian style, Georgian style etc.).

THE CZECH REPUBLIC

After the First World War, Czechoslovakia became an independent state. The decades between 1920 and 1940, witnessed various concurrent movements in Czech architecture: a nationalist revival style, a monumental style influenced by the German and Russian dictatorships, as well as a modern style that was a blend, partly, of Franco-German Purism and of Russian Constructivism, in particular. The architect, Josef Chochol (1880–1956) was a forerunner, having experienced the Cubist era, he then moved on to embrace absolute Purism.

Constructivism prevailed during the 1920s in Czechoslovakia: high-rise buildings, compact volumes mostly destined for offices were articulated by alternating stringcourses and plate glass. The prevailing motto was, 'Ornament is unnecessary: construction defines form'. Some of these buildings were built in the historic city centre of Prague, such as Jindrich Svoboda's Bata Building in Wenceslas Square (1929), encased entirely in glass, or Ludvik Kysela's Alfa Palace and Tatran Hotel, of the same period. From 1930 onwards, Functionalism was infused with greater international influence and the composition of volumes was simplified. An example of this simplification is Josef Gocar's Church of St Wenceslas (1933) in the Vršovice district, which has a stepped nave and a high tower on the façade. The church was reminiscent of Dutch architecture and the General Pensions Institute building (1928) — now the House of Trade Unions. Many schools of the new government were designed in the Functionalist style, while Soviet Constructivism continued to influence designs for residential buildings. Residential districts were built on the outskirts of Prague, similar to a garden-city suburb, designed according to Modern Movement principles. The most well-known of these is the Baba Housing Estate on the hill overlooking the Castle.

Josef Havlicek and Karel Honzik, General Pensions Institute (now the House of Trade Unions), 1928, Prague
Rather than adhering to the design criteria prescribed by the brief for the building on the perimeter of the city block with a central courtyard, the two young architects planned the layout as an innovative cruciform. The design is reminiscent of some of Le Corbusier's major works: two intersecting volumes of different heights with horizontal strip windows. The General Pensions Institute remains the most important example of Functionalist architecture in the Czech Republic.

Villa (top), (left) Baba Housing Estate, 1933, Prague

The Baba garden-housing estate, built on the hills in Prague, is comprised of thirty-three villas. To this day the housing estate remains the most significant legacy of the Modern Movement in the Czech Republic. The estate was built by local architects, unknown internationally, all of who were extremely well-versed in Functionalism. The complex incorporates the entire spectrum of the Modern lexicon: pure white volumes with loggias, cantilevered roofs, strip windows and flat roofs.

ART DECO

The Exposition des Arts Décoratifs et Industriels Modernes (International Exhibition of Modern Decorative and Industrial Arts), which celebrated the first twenty-five years of the 20th century — and the return of peace — opened in Paris in 1925. The expo was a response to the demands of artists and industrialists that had called for an expo since 1915. It encompassed a broad variety of themes: there was the Purist pavilion of the Esprit Nouveau (Le Corbusier and Ozenfant), the garden with tree-like Cubist sculptures, eclectic pavilions that were influenced by folklore as well as, in particular, a new decorative style that was named after the exhibition: Art Deco. The movement was inspired by a desire for decoration in its own right, with no particular functional purpose. The architects strove to create a greater urban impact than Rationalist Minimalism, with bulkier, more expressive shapes; towers and stepped roofs like ziggurats. Every visible element was decorated: cornices, ceilings, lintels, doorways, corner junctions etc. To distinguish Art Deco from the naturalist Art Nouveau, the decoration was geometric and abstract: stripes, small squares, triangles, zigzags, on occasion with the addition of cornices and corbels. Colours were generally used, with every possible hue and unusual combinations of colours. Every surface was filled with classically or naturalistically inspired reliefs (Greek divinities, gazelles or female figures). Art Deco decoration was homogenous, regardless of scale, from utensils to skyscrapers. It tended to be made from newly developed materials such as aluminium and Bakelite. Art Deco had numerous sources of inspiration: from the geometry of the Werkbund (the German movement that encompassed Rationalist artisans and architects) to Greek, Egyptian and Aztek motifs; from the forms of Cubism to the strong colours of the Fauves. However, what made a strong impact was the extraordinary influence the movement had with its instantly recognisable shapes. These were the *Années Folles* of a widely disseminated style that had helped to promote a general understanding of Rationalism internationally.

opposite page
Robert Mallet Stevens, design for the Tourist Pavilion, 1925, Exposition des Arts Décoratifs et Industriels Modernes, Paris
Mallet Stevens, an architect who designed Cubist-inspired houses, submitted a design for a cruciform tower adorned with repeated projecting appliqué planes that were purely decorative.

Pierre Patout, Collector's Pavilion garden façade, 1925, Exposition des Arts Décoratifs et Industriels Modernes, Paris
This design by Pierre Patout fragments the volume and surfaces into separate geometric elements: the ziggurat-style stepped roof, the protruding zigzag bands and the slanting, asymmetrical entry. This design epitomises the new Art Deco code.

CLASSICISM AND ECLECTICISM

Modern Movement architecture was by no means universally admired. Its vocabulary was regarded by some as being sterile; it seemed to lack historical references and was therefore generally disparaged. Hence the survival of several forms of Eclecticism that endured for the decades between 1920 and 1940. Neo-Gothic architecture had two areas where is could be applied: churches — it was the style used in many great cathedrals — and skyscrapers, due to their vertical thrust. In Neo-Gothic architecture, unlike the architecture of the Modern Movement, mullions were left visible between the glass panes i.e. windows were not abstracted. The example that best illustrates the Neo-Gothic style was Peder Vilhelm Jensen-Klint's (1853–1930), Grundtvig Church in Copenhagen (1921–1926) where the façade is designed to resemble a pipe-organ. Neo-Palladianism became extremely popular in England. Its aesthetic was used for houses and palaces as well as for projects like Regent Street in London (1922), built by the British architect Reginald Blomfield (1856–1942).

Jensen Klint, Grundtvig Church, 1921–1926, Copenhagen
Klint's design won a competition in 1913, but the project was only built many years later between 1921 and 1926. The façade and western section are higher than the nave. The design was conceived as a pipe-organ interpreted in a Neo-Gothic manner. A symbolically triangular Gothic pediment incorporated the three entry doors.

The most widespread architectural style however, was Neo-Classical. Neo-Classicism was frequently used for the palaces of the ruling élite in Europe: Germany, Spain and occasionally in Italy, as well as in the Soviet Union. It was the style chosen for the great colonial projects such as the Viceroy's Palace and the government buildings in New Delhi, designed by Edwin Lutyens (1912–1931). Neo-Classicism was also the style of choice for several new buildings in democratic countries like the United States. For example, Henry Bacon's (1911–1922) Lincoln Memorial in Washington; the capital city that was aspired the architectural aesthetic of classical Rome or Athens.

The architect who was able to interpret Neo-Classical Revival most poetically was the Slovenian, Jože Plečnik, who studied under Otto Wagner until 1910. After the rigorously Secessionist period, Plečnik was able to apply his rigorous approach to Neo-Classical Revival to Monumentalism as well. This is suggested by the quality of space and multiple orders of columns, as in the hall that bears his name in Prague Castle (1926–1928), as well as the interior of the Church of St Francis in Ljubljana (1925–1928). The monumental entrance to the Zale Cemetery in Ljubljana (1937–1940) recalls the scenography of Roman theatres, with a double-order portico opening onto a central exedra. The outbreak of the Second World War put a halt to these stylistic trends.

Henry Bacon, Lincoln Memorial, 1911–1922, Washington
The Neo-Classical mausoleum, which encompasses the statue of Abraham Lincoln, consists of a white marble sarcophagus, surrounded by an elegant Doric colonnade, which is reminiscent of a Greek temple without its tympanum. The Lincoln Memorial is situated close to a Neo-Egyptian obelisk and the Capitol, which was clearly inspired by the Renaissance. The architecture was designed to imbue the newly-built city of Washington with historical gravitas.

JOŽE PLEČNIK

After studying and serving an apprenticeship in Vienna, Jože Plečnik (1872–1957) returned to his home city, Ljubljana. The architect moved to Prague in order to take up a teaching post in 1920 and also in order to design the external spaces and some of the internal rooms for the Castle, which was due to become the headquarters of the newly-formed state government. Plečnik designed the courtyards, the front garden known as the Paradise and the Bastion of rear garden, along with a few of the rooms. Plečnik had already abandoned the Viennese Secessionist figurative language in 1910, whilst working on the Church of the Holy Spirit in Vienna. He designed a façade for the church similar to a Doric temple. The architect was formulating a vocabulary that included classical elements such as water basins, echini, columns, plinths and balustrades, which he designed on a huge scale and pared down to a token form, classically sober and enormously elegant. He constructed the church using precious materials such as marble, brass and copper. The materials adorned the great open spaces and articulated his rigorous compositions which surprised with their unexpected asymmetries. The space known as 'Plečnik Hall' is rather like a covered Roman peristyle, with a triple order of white columns, positioned in front of the white perimeter wall. The hall is a classical space — a forerunner of Post-Modernism — enclosed with a timber coffered ceiling. The gardens feature some isolated pieces of architecture that demarcate the landscape; even the trees were arranged in a geometric design. Critics initially failed to understand Plečnik 's architecture, which was only rediscovered relatively recently, during the 1980s.

opposite page
Jože Plečnik, Castle interior, 1926–1928, Prague.
The space is conceived as a covered Roman peristyle with a triple order of columns, featuring simplified, geometric design elements, rhythmic and symmetrical. The sombre lighting enhances the metaphysical quality of the space.

below
Jože Plečnik, garden view, 1926–1928, Prague
A sculptural curved staircase deriving from Sebastiano Serlio's 16th century handbook leads into the garden, which has a classical composition inspired by French landscaping.

THE UNITED STATES
1920—1940

During the 1920s, the urban population of the United States consisted largely of European immigrants. This obviously affected the kind of architecture produced there, which tended to be rather eclectic, nostalgically echoing the architectural styles of the myriad homelands of the immigrants. Modern architecture took some time to take hold in the new world and was imported to the United States from Europe. The jury for the competition to build the Tribune Tower in 1922 chose (yet another) Neo-Gothic building from the hundreds of entries it received from all over the world.

The first significant move toward modernising architecture in the United States only began during the late 1930s. During a period of slow recovery after the 1929 economic crisis, there were only two significant urban models: highly developed cities, with high-rise office blocks and compact, single-family houses designed in a traditional manner. The development of the suburbs paved the way for the creation of new garden cities based on Ebenezer Howard's urban plans and his concepts for creating open green areas in cities. Frank Lloyd Wright was unique in terms of the quantity of his production and the quality of his architecture. Wright went through a Californian Neo-Mayan phase during the 1920s; followed by a few years of inactivity until the 1930s when he resurfaced again to produce a number of architectural masterpieces. Two of these gems include: Fallingwater and the Johnson Wax Building. Other important architectural works were carried out by Rudolph Schindler and Richard Neutra, who were both based in California. Neutra designed Rationalist single-family houses influenced by the ordered rationality of Japanese architecture; which had a fundamental impact on the development of the Californian School. Eliel Saarinen, who emigrated to the United States from Finland in 1923, won the second prize in the Chicago Tribune competition. Saarinen designed buildings according to Classical principles which he applied specifically to public buildings; an exemplary project is his Cranbrook Academy in Michigan, where he taught.

Frank Lloyd Wright, Johnson Wax Building
interior, 1950, Racine, Wisconsin

THE CHICAGO TRIBUNE COMPETITION

The Chicago Tribune newspaper launched a competition to build its new headquarters in 1922, for the princely sum of 100,000 dollars for the prize-winning design. This was the first competition of its kind to be held for the first skyscraper in Chicago's rapidly expanding city. Hundreds of designs were submitted by a wide cross-section of architects. The winning architects, John Mead Howells (1868 1959) and Raymond Hood (1881–1934) designed a Neo-Gothic high-rise tower, which became a prototype design for skyscrapers all over the United States. The architecture of the new typology of vertical building was eclectic; the buildings were held by buttresses, like the naves of cathedrals.

Gropius and Meyer both submitted a design for a tower consisting of volumes of varying heights with the entire structural frame visible, whilst a few corner balconies break up the façade. The tower was a Rationalist interpretation of the Chicago style, also employing the proportion and design of Chicago windows. Max Taut submitted a Rationalist design which had a façade that was articulated with a chequered lattice, whilst Jan Duiker's building had great horizontal bands, alternately opaque and transparent as was typical of his Dutch projects. The European masters were seemingly unprepared for the high standard of work expected by the jurors and approached the competition as if it were merely a sketch design exercise. Loos submitted a skyscraper in the shape of a free-standing Doric column, which critics assumed was meant to be ironic. In actual fact Loos, who had often employed classical columns in his designs, believed that the cultural branding of a newspaper of that calibre could be symbolised by that particular shape, and that the extraordinary large-scale high-rise would be capable of becoming an iconic symbol rather like the Eiffel Tower. Other, less well-known architects also designed skyscrapers in the form of a column. Eliel Saarinen was awarded the second prize with his ziggurat-shaped tower. His design combined Classical, Gothic and historic Romantic elements and turned out to be the design that was to be most frequently imitated right up to the 1940s. A group of Italian architects, including Marcello Piacentini, also entered the competition for the high-rise though their design submissions were of inferior quality. Wright, who was not interested in competing against others, was conspicuous in his absence.

opposite page
John Mead Howells and Raymond Hood, Chicago Tribune, 1922, Chicago, Illinois
The Chicago Tribune is an example of Neo-Gothic, New York style and demonstrates the fact that the committee was definitely biased against innovative architectural styles. The upper section of the building, with its projecting buttresses, borrows ideals from French cathedrals.

left
Adolf Loos, entry design for the Chicago Tribune Tower competition, 1922
Loos' massive Doric column is a kind of manifesto or symbol of culture and tradition, filled with Classical as well as critical stylistic elements. His design was by no means the only entry to feature a design in the form of a Doric or Egyptian column.

right
Eliel Saarinen, entry design for the Chicago Tribune Tower competition, 1922
Eliel Saarinen's stepped skyscraper combines various different stylistic influences, deriving from his earlier Romantic buildings in Finland and later from the influence of his experiences in the United States. Saarinen's design was more Americanised and more synthetically simplified than the others, and was to become a prototype for many more skyscrapers in the United States.

RICHARD NEUTRA

The Austrian architect, Richard Neutra (1892–1970), was in a league of his own in the history of contemporary architecture. This was due to his unstinting and committed professional career, his ability to integrate architecture and nature, the technical and formal quality of his designs, his grasp of American culture and the achievement of his enormous volume of work. Although he cannot be classed as one of the truly great masters, Neutra designed high-quality houses. However, his designs were often rather similar to one another; he did not really explore new avenues. Neutra came into contact with several famous architects during his training; he studied Otto Wagner's work in Austria and maintained that he was inspired to become an architect after his meeting with Adolf Loos in 1910. Neutra and Mendelsohn won the competition for the Business Centre in Haifa in 1923, which was never realised. Neutra emigrated to Chicago that same year — believing the United States to be the promised land — where he met Wright and worked in his studio from 1925 onwards. In 1927 Neutra started working in Los Angeles, mostly designing schools and single-family dwellings, although he was also a consultant to the

Richard Neutra, Lovell House (Health House), 1927–1929, Los Angeles, California

Lovell House was built into a hillside, with access from above. There are three projecting floors with windows overlooking the cityscape: a compact garden with a swimming pool. The house has a Rationalist design applied to an articulated volume, white finishes, large apertures and a landscaped exterior space. It was this project that established Neutra's stylistic principles and established his reputation.

Social Housing Board (from 1931) and Chairman of the California City Planning Commission as he had a special interest in urban issues. Neutra's vocabulary was rigorously Rationalist, although he treated space holistically: his volumes were orthogonal, assembled in various different compositions, their construction pared down to their steel-framed structures (steel was used in order to be able to preserve slender proportions), with continuous, sliding glazed walls. Neutra liked to provide an integral sacred area around his buildings and he designed the outside spaces with great attention. He landscaped swimming pools, pergolas, lawns and shrubs. Internally, Neutra was also fastidious; designing all the furnishings himself. One can detect the influence of Japanese architecture as well as traces of Le Corbusier and Wright's ideas in Neutra's work. The architect had a singular and fresh approach for the 1930s; he was able to design within a new world context, free from the weight of architectural history. Neutra remained faithful to his approach consistently into the 1960s; he had a profound influence on Californian architecture.

Richard Neutra, Miller House, 1937, Palm Springs, California
Miller House is a compact, orthogonal house, completely open to the surrounding countryside. The lounge area opens onto a small swimming pool. The interior can be partitioned by sliding walls; reminiscent of Japanese architecture.

RUDOLPH SCHINDLER

Rudolph Schindler, Schindler House, exterior, 1922, Los Angeles, California

Schindler's first built project was his own residence, which was a two-unit dwelling. The design concept was to integrate the interior and exterior as far as possible: thus creating a very structured layout. Each room has a glazed wall which opens onto one of the internal gardens. The influence of domestic Japanese architecture is clear: in the use of timber, the contained spaces, the sliding screen walls and ochre plasterwork in order to achieve an atmosphere of minimalist intimacy. Schindler's influence on Californian residential architecture was so profound that the house has now been made open to the public.

It was two Austrian-born architects, Richard Neutra and Rudolph Schindler — both of whom studied under Adolf Loos in Vienna — that triggered the vogue for single-family dwellings and the figurative Rationalist approach to architecture in California. Schindler (1887–1953) was fascinated by his master's recollections of life in Chicago and decided to move to the United States in 1914, finding employment in Chicago. Schindler joined Wright's studio in 1917, at a time when Wright was spending a lot of time in Japan, and was thus able to follow the development of several projects for single-family dwellings from beginning to end. In 1920 he travelled to Los Angeles to oversee the building of Barnsdall House where he decided to set up his own private practice. Los Angeles seemed like a paradise, where he could be free to produce his own personal concept of architecture. The internal and external spaces had to be given equal importance: life could be led outside or inside a building equally. Houses had to be absolutely site-specific and each room had to have at least one glazed wall. In order to achieve this, Schindler's plans were very structured; they were informed by extremely meticulous research. His œuvre consisted of single-family houses and small-scale residential schemes. He reduced his spaces into their constituent units, so that each could be independent. Schindler's vocabulary was influenced by Japanese architecture: compact spaces, sliding screen walls, subdivision of windowpanes into squares and slatted sun-blinds. He designed all the furnishings internally as taught by Loos, making great use of timber and built-in furniture. The first house Schindler ever built, was built for himself in 1922; this design was more permeated with Japanese elements than any of his other houses; his later designs were more Rationalist and De Stijl influenced. Examples of this are his Oliver and Buck Houses (1933), both built in Los Angeles. The Wolfe House, built in 1928 on Catalina Island, was composed of superimposed, staggered terraces, overlooking the ocean. Schindler's architectural direction was to continue along the same path, in some instances employing Neutra's vocabulary, in others, a more holistic approach.

WRIGHT AND THE KAUFMANN HOUSE

Kaufmann House, better known as 'Fallingwater', is situated in Bear Run, Pennsylvania. The site is a steep slope in a dense forest leading down to a river and a small waterfall. The house was conceived as two deep, horizontal volumes perpendicular to one another, seemingly suspended without support above the rock face. The large terraces link the volumes together and define them. The result is deliberately overwhelming; the architectural elements are extremely powerful and play on the tension created by suspension. Wright produced a feat of bold technical engineering, incorporated imperceptibly into the form of the house.

There are few distinct elements, used to different dramatic effect: a vertical stone tower (chimney) acts as a counterpoint to the horizontal thrust of the terraces, ochre-coloured plaster and grey stone, solid walls and floor-to-ceiling windows. The interior consists of compact spaces, each with its own deep terrace; in contrast, the living room is an enormous, horizontal space, enclosed to the hillside but also thrust open towards the valley.

Fallingwater is built along Prairie House principles: the hearth is the focal point of the house, although in this case it is situated in a corner position and features in more than one room. The horizontal floors are conspicuous by their sheer size; bands of floor-to-ceiling windows provide magnificent views to the exterior landscape and wall planes and volumes are articulated according to orthogonal axes. The building is a paradigm of 1930s Organic Architecture, with elements arranged in a regular, yet unstructured manner and dictated by their functions and the symbiosis of architecture and nature. Wright's success in fusing the two extremes: formal and poetic, produced a unique work, unparalleled in the history of contemporary architecture.

Frank Lloyd Wright, Kaufmann House (or Fallingwater), exterior view, 1936–1939, Bear Run, Pennsylvania
After a lengthy period of professional inactivity, Wright marked his return to architecture with a masterpiece: a country home for the Kaufmann family who owned a department store in Pittsburgh. The house straddles a waterfall in a forest, hence its nickname 'Fallingwater'. The building is composed of deep terraces and horizontal cantilevered levels set in contrast to a vertical stone tower. The terraces project so far out that the façades of the house are obscured from the outside. The interior is well planned, with compact rooms on several floors, each room with its own terrace; there is a generous sitting room, which fluidly intertwines the interior of the house with the exterior landscape.

WRIGHT AND TALIESIN WEST

Wright never took up a post as an academic in a university; he did however build two architecture schools during his career. Students were able to gain work experience with Wright on these projects. The first school, Taliesin East, on the great Wisconsin plain, his home territory, was unfortunately partly destroyed by fire. The second school, Taliesin West, was built in the Arizona Desert in 1937, not far from the state capital, Phoenix. It was a deliberate choice to site the school in the desert, at a distance from the urban world. As it accommodated a studio as well as a residential school, the school consisted of several buildings designed in the architectural vocabulary typical of Wright's latter period. The buildings have unusual lines, irregular triangles on slanted supports, rhythmically repeated, creating an effect rather like the exposed vertebrae of the pavilions; overtly pointed shapes that he reincorporated in some of his Usonian houses and in his later works. The buildings have timber structures with stone piers using local materials. Furthermore, there were two water features on the polygonal perimeter, one orientated towards the interior and the other orientated towards the exterior, in accordance with the principle of the co-existence of natural elements with human-made structures. The architectural space was supposed to represent the air, the desert the earth and the hearth, fire. Wright interpreted architecture through his organic principles that informed his design and the forms that shaped it.

opposite page
Frank Lloyd Wright, interior of the studio (top) and a detail of the Taliesin West pavilions, 1937, Scottsdale, Arizona

Frank Lloyd Wright, view of Taliesin West, 1937, Scottsdale, Arizona
The architecture of Taliesin West is low-slung and extends across the desert. The carefully structured building encompasses a courtyard which opens out to one side, as well as a water feature. The larger spaces are articulated by a series of open supporting structures; the trapezoidal section provide visual dynamic and allow directional light to illuminate the space from one side.

ART DECO IN THE UNITED STATES

It is logical that the United States, having been colonised by Europeans, would be drawn to the traditional European styles (Gothic, Baroque, Palladian etc.) that they were familiar with for their representative buildings. It was the new generation of architects who gradually imported the latest trends from the Continent. Art Deco enjoyed unexpected, yet instant, success, proving even more popular than in Europe after 1925. Under President Roosevelt's New Deal reforms, post-1929, the movement enjoyed even greater popularity and success. It was also referred to as 'Streamline Modern' or 'Jazz Age' in cultural circles. The figurative canons of Art Deco were more extreme than in Europe and were sometimes even combined with other stylistic elements, where decoration and colour were taken to the limit. There are still over one thousand Art Deco buildings in the United States, primarily situated in New York, Los Angeles, Washington and Miami. There are, however a far greater number of buildings that have Art Deco detailing: there are no shortage of applications: doors, frescoes, bas-reliefs, carvings, furnishings and lamps. There is an entire 'Deco District' in Miami, running parallel to the beach, where there are small multi-coloured buildings that have been restructured and trans-

Wurdeman and Becket, Pan Pacific Auditorium, 1935, Los Angeles, California
The Pan Pacific Auditorium was a kind of compendium of Art Deco: four strange, curiously-shaped towers anchor a curved entry portico decorated with strong horizontal planes and bold colours. Unfortunately, following a fire in 1989, the building was demolished and the site was utilised as a parking lot once again.

formed several times. Overall, the street front resembles dinky toytown. During the 1920s film boom in Los Angeles, Art Deco style was employed widely for residences, offices, film studios and theatres all over the city. Film sets of the period were inspired by Art Deco and helped to popularise it internationally. In the United States in particular, there was a widespread vogue for decoration and the inclusion of special features, such as spires, pinnacles and statues, such as, for example, the famous Chrysler Building in New York, which displays a superb blend of Gothic and Art Deco elements. Other examples include the Ritz Plaza in Miami and the Bullocks Wilshire in Los Angeles.

left
John and Donald Parkinson, Bullocks Wilshire Department Store, 1929, Los Angeles, California
The tower is the focal point of the Bullocks Wilshire Department Store building (now the Southwestern Law School). The tower is crowned with a copper volume that thrusts upwards from the lower section of the tower. The ensemble resembles a mausoleum, consisting of various elements and decorated with copper-plated, zigzag parapets.

below
Murray Dixon, Ritz Plaza Hotel, 1940, Miami, Florida
This hotel in Miami is an example of late Art Deco architecture. It is exemplary in its use of plastic masses as well as its use of subtle different shades of a single colour.

SKYSCRAPERS

Skyscrapers were developed in the United States and remain one of the country's most emblematic inventions. As the name suggests, skyscrapers are extremely tall and bold buildings. Their construction was made possible by technological progress in steel structures and the invention of the lift. Further catalysts were: limitless land exploitation, corporate branding and the desire for high-rise buildings able to accommodate a huge number of workspaces, thereby achieving maximum urban density. Skyscrapers embodied the antithesis of the American aspiration to own single-family dwellings in green neighbourhoods. This ambition was fed by the nostalgia immigrants had to create their own homelands as well as their pioneering expectations. The simplicity of the structure and the geometric layout of skyscrapers freed the design of the façades. Thus a new generation of buildings emerged which did not have a great historical legacy. Architects designed them as they thought fit and any style was seen to be acceptable. Neo-Gothic style was particularly popular because it emphasised the verticality of the high-risers, but Renaissance and Mayan elements were also employed, in some instances with Greek, Roman or Romanesque details, or even an eclectic blend of all three, with little or no reference to the latest architectural trends in Europe. Therefore, it was hardly surprising that the jurors of the competition for the Chicago Tribune Tower (1922) chose the Neo-Gothic design submitted by John Mead Howells and Raymond Hood amongst the hundreds of submissions. Hood had also designed the American Radiator Building (New York, 1924), which displayed a combination of Gothic and Romanesque styles and was decorated and colourful. Due to building regulations, the volumes were stepped, rather like a tall ziggurat. The design of a skyscraper needed to address three particular issues: how the junction of the building and the ground functioned, how the façade was treated and how the apex was articulated. The Rockefeller Center (New York, 1932) was a complex of homogenous volumes of varying heights; the architect resolved the ground-junction issue with a sunken piazza to distinguish it from the surrounding flat ground plane. The façade

Raymond Hood, Wallace Kirkman Harrison, Rockefeller Center, 1932, New York
The Rockefeller Center is a building complex which has a central skyscraper and several identical satellite buildings. The scheme absorbs several city blocks and has a central piazza, which sets it apart and distinguishes it from the monotonous urban fabric surrounding it. The austere façade was designed like an abstract painting with square windows framed by horizontal and vertical bands, reminiscent of paintings by the artists, Mondrian and Albers.

was extraordinarily progressive for that time: it has square windows set between slender vertical bands. The cinematic façade of the iconic Chrysler Building (New York, 1929) has a sophisticated design, with delicate Viennese elements and a magnificent Art Deco/Gothic spire which is adorned with radial decorations clad in a shiny metallic skin. The Empire State Building (New York, 1931), which was the tallest skyscraper at that time, has a phallic spire above an Aztec pyramid.

The PSFS Building by George Howe and William Lescaze (Philadelphia, 1932) indicated a radical change of style: here there was an assembly of orthogonal volumes of differing heights assembled asymmetrically. Up until 1940, there was a fall in the number of new skyscrapers built due to the Great Crash of 1929. The PSFS high-rise served as a prototype for designs after 1950.

CITIES AND LARGE-SCALE PROJECTS

From 1930 onwards, Europe was faced with the issue of social housing. Most European countries found themselves in a similar situation: populations were becoming more urbanised and housing needed to be supplied en masse for all. This was the era of the great urban plans and large building projects. Every nation had its own particular solution to the housing problem: solutions specific to each context.

In Germany, the *'Siedlungen'* or settlements were rigorously geometric with parallel housing blocks, orientated optimally for daylight. The blocks were medium density, low-rise (four floors high without lifts) with amenities situated in one of the residential blocks or in purpose-built blocks. The German housing model was also adopted in Italy, the Netherlands, France and Switzerland.

Austria, however, tended to built large-scale, enclosed complexes. The housing estates were capable of accommodating hundreds of families; the blocks were not orientated in any particular direction and the social mix was regarded as being more important than aesthetics. The complexes provided for some primary services within the complex (nurseries, doctor's surgeries, leisure clubs etc.). This housing typology was subsequently employed in large schemes in Eastern European countries.

Bruno Taut, aerial view of Siedlung Britz,
1925–1931, Berlin

In the Soviet Union, urban planners were experimenting with an altogether differ-ent building typology, termed 'Dom Kommuna'. This urban housing concept con-sisted of massive concrete blocks, as can be seen in Ivanowo or Moscow — where vast 300-metre-high buildings were constructed. Enormous cruciform buildings were developed containing communal services (laundry, gym, communal rooms etc.), which meant that the apartments could be kept small, according to the prin-ciple of Soviet advanced collectivism.

In the Netherlands, housing schemes were also based on the German model. Some of the social schemes consisted of ten-storey blocks arranged around gal-leries as promoted by Gropius. The first attempts at prefabrication were also made. These building schemes, along with the Soviet Dom Kommuna complexes, marked the transition towards Le Corbusier's post-War 'Housing Units'.

France adopted the highly dense neighbourhood schemes of Germany, with high buildings ('Villeurbanne') or, as in Le Rancy, schemes built using innovative tech-niques (steel structures, prefabricated materials etc.)

England, which was removed from the European scene, only built a few schemes that were noteworthy in terms of the zoning of urban space.

For the first time in architectural history the most renowned architects in Europe (and in some instances, internationally) organised annual conferences in order to debate universal principles on fundamental issues: from city centres to housing, restoration to planning. Thanks to Le Corbusier's unflagging energy, in 1925, nine years after the end of the War as the great urban projects were being developed, twenty-four architects founded the CIAM or International Congresses of Modern Architecture. This enabled architects who belonged to the Modern Movement to keep up contact with one another internationally and to disseminate their ideas in order to define their urban planning and architectural objectives with regard to improving social quality on a global scale. The architects that attended the confer-ence included the Frenchmen, Pierre Chareau and Jean Lurçat, the Germans, Ernst May and Hugo Häring, the Dutchmen, Gerrit Rietveld and Mart Stam, the Swiss, Karl Moser, the Austrian, Josef Frank and the Italians, Carlo Enrico Rava and Alberto Sartoris. The first Secretary of the CIAM was the renowned critic and his-torian, Sigfried Giedion (1888–1968). The new architectural trends that had emerged from the beginning of the century and the early 1920S were disrupted by a global initiative that was to recruit the likes of Alvar Aalto, Richard Neutra, Kunio

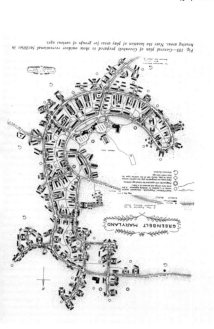

above, left
Various authors, Neubühl district, 1930, Zurich, Switzerland
This large district on the slopes of Zurich was meticulously laid out, with neat rows of parallel blocks. The indi-vidual units were designed with partic-ular attention to detail. Gardens and allotments were arranged in order to maximise the use of space and func-tionality. Thus a pleasant environment was created despite the high-density grid of buildings situated in close proximity to one another.

above, right
Clarence Stein, floor plan, 1933, Greenbelt, Maryland
This garden-city suburb was designed in a crescent shape, to tie into the sur-rounding landscape, with vehicular roads on the periphery and narrower internal roads leading to the residential areas. The civic building is located cen-trally and accommodates the town hall, schools and the library. The sur-rounding forested area was left as a green belt.

Fig. 105—General plan of Greenbelt to show outdoor recreational facilities in housing areas. Note the location of play areas for groups of various ages.

CIAM, group photo of those at the first Meeting, 1928, La Sarraz, Switzerland
From left to right, top row: Mart Stam, Max Ernst Haefeli, Rudolf Steiger, Hans Schmidt, Paul Artaria, Frederich Gubler; next row down: Richard Dupierreux, Pierre Chareau, Victor Bourgeois, Ernst May (hidden), Hugo Häring, Juan De Zavala, Lucienne Florentin, Le Corbusier, Hélène De Mandrot, Rochat, André Lurçat, Henri-Robert von der Mühll, Gino Maggioni, Huibrecht Hoste, Sigfried Giedion, Werner Max Moser, Josef Franke; third row from the top: Pierre Jeanneret, Gerrit Rietveld, Alberto Sartoris, Gabriel Guevrekian, Fernando García Mercadal (seated), Weber Tadevassian.

Mayekawa and Oscar Niemeyer, spreading as far as Japan and India in the East and the United States and Cuba in the West. The conferences were held on a more or less annual basis: each one producing a manifesto. The first meeting was held in 1928 in La Sarraz, Switzerland. There, the general principles of architecture and modern urbanism were drawn up by Le Corbusier and Gropius. The theme for the following year was 'Existenzminimum' ('subsistence housing'). The conference was held in Frankfurt, where the subsistence-housing model was being put to trial. In 1930, the CIAM met in Brussels, where Dutch concepts were analysed; the theme was residential typology: 'high' versus 'low' housing. In 1933 the delegates travelled by boat from Marseilles to Athens to formulate the Athens Charter: a manifesto that focused on the characteristics of modern cities, which was drawn up after with after many days of hard work during the journey. In 1937, the CIAM organised an exhibition geared to spreading the word in Prague. The meetings continued during the post-war period, but were finally officially disbanded after the eleventh conference in Ottowa Otterlo, held in 1959.

GERMANY

Urban social housing was the largest production sector in Germany during the economic crisis between 1920 and 1930. A decision was made to build large-scale socially homogenous and economically sustainable districts. The urban plan only provided for open-plan buildings configured in parallel lines, orientated on the north-south axis in order to optimise sunlight. There were few variations to this layout. Blocks were not enclosed and there were no courtyards: the local amenities were sited in purpose-built spaces. A number of double-storey blocks were also built, but they were generally four storeys high (the maximum permissible without a lift). Gropius submitted an unsuccessful design for a ten or eleven-storey-high block. The scale and the distribution of the housing were crucial aspects: during the 1929 CIAM conference in Frankfurt, Alexander Klein inserted the various studies together into the smallest habitable space (*Existenzminimum*) and drew up standards for room dimensions and for the space:inhabitant ratio for the very first time. Architectural handbooks were published, which illustrated every possible type of information regarding dimensions and ergonomic function. Hygiene regulations also had to be applied. Each room had to have fresh air and every dwelling had to have a lavatory. The biggest housing schemes, overseen by Bruno Taut, were built in Berlin between 1924 and 1933. There were a few exemplary projects such as the Siedlung Britz (1925–1931), which had a central horseshoe-shaped block and Siemensstadt (1929–1932) designed by Scharoun.
A further important group of housing estates were built on the northern outskirts of Frankfurt. In around 1930 a type of housing estate, each with its own allotment and geared to self-sufficiency, was favoured. This was the preferred Nazi housing settlement.

Hans Scharoun, view of a Siemensstadt housing block, 1929–1932, Berlin
Scharoun, who designed the urban layout for the district, also planned three separate houses, one arched and two U-shaped, situated close to the underpass to the south of the railway. All three houses are the same height, i.e. low enough to dispense with the need for a lift. In accordance with Rationalist criteria, the buildings are all white with flat roofs, but are enlivened by Scharoun's trademark curved balconies.

GROPIUS AND THE LARGE-SCALE ESTATES

Gropius left the Bauhaus in 1928 in order to return to his architectural practice: from then on he concentrated almost exclusively on social housing, researching methods of prefabrication as well as the standardisation of dimensioning and component parts.

The first housing estate he built was in Törten, Dessau (1926–1928) and consisted of rows of low, double-storey, white, flat-roofed buildings. These were modest constructions, of interest as an example of a building system with a regimented urban layout. In 1928, Gropius won a competition to design low-rise housing in Karlsruhe. The scheme, known as the Dammerstock, was laid out in strictly parallel lines. Thereafter he began to work on four and five-storey buildings, which he then built in Celle, followed by the three Siemensstadt buildings in Berlin (1930) that were a set of identical white blocks. In order to enliven the elevations, Gropius inserted matching pairs of balconies on one façade and demarcated the division between the component housing modules on the opposite façade. Meanwhile, he was also developing his much replicated ten to eleven-storey high-rise block which was to form the basis for the Wannsee Complex in Berlin (1931). Unfortunately, the complex never developed beyond planning phase. Gropius also played an active role in the CIAM, second only to Le Corbusier. He presented his theoretical research on housing at CIAM conferences. After his emigration from Germany with the rise of Nazism (1933), Gropius abandoned his research on social housing.

Walter Gropius, façades of housing blocks in the Siemensstadt, 1930, Berlin
Gropius built three, four-storey blocks, repeating the same basic housing unit. Despite his abundant research, the buildings were nevertheless constructed using traditional techniques.

THE 'HÖFE' COURTYARDS IN VIENNA

Between 1920 and 1933, Vienna had a Socialist government and was known as 'Rote Wien' (Red Vienna). It was a metropolis with excellent services but lacked social housing. The urban renewal planned, was intended to provide this social housing. With special legislation and funding, 70, 000 dwellings were built to house approximately 300, 000 people: 10% of the population lived in council housing, the *Gemeindebauten.* The estates were largely located along the Ring, the site of the former city walls, on land that, for military reasons, had historically been state property. The project was to provide large housing estates, blocks echoing the 19th century vision of neighbourhood units, each housing hundreds — if not thousands — of families. The designs borrowed heavily from Viennese architectural tradition with introverted complexes built around a central courtyard *(Hof),* which served as the heart of the estate, a collective area, or garden, equipped with various communal amenities: nursery school, baths, health centre etc.

Hubert Gessner, Karl Seitz Hof, 1924–1926, Vienna
Gessner sought to create a strong characteristic image for these working class homes. In this case, a semicircular shape was chosen reminiscent of the English crescents, with two rectilinear wings embracing the central green courtyard or *Hof.*

The *Höfe* schemes were high-density; the architecture made no reference to the Modern Movement, but was based on the Viennese School, with a powerful figurative character conveying nobility and urban gravitas for the working-class housing. The most notable example is the Winarsky Hof (1926) by Peter Behrens. Josef Hoffmann, Josef Frank and others also designed linear building blocks with a circulation spine running between them. Further examples are the crescent-shaped, Karl Seitz Hof (1926), the large complex around Engelsplatz (1933) which has a square courtyard and two towers symmetrical to the entrance. The Karl Marx Hof (1930) is the most representative of all Viennese housing schemes. Construction of the *Höfe* came to a halt with the advent of Nazism, but the model served as a prototype for a great many council estates throughout the Soviet Union between 1933 and 1953.

Engelsplatz, 1933, Vienna
This courtyard complex has two powerful, symmetrical entrances. While it borrows from Viennese tradition, the complex also has echoes of Rationalism.

THE MASTERPIECE
KARL MARX HOF

The Karl Marx Hof is the most representative 'Red Vienna' scheme in terms of scale and figurative elements. The scheme was designed by the municipal architect, Karl Ehn (1884–1959), who was the first *'Siedlung'* (i.e. schemes with rows of low houses) architect in Austria. Ehn was also responsible for producing other public buildings under Nazi occupation. The Karl Marx Hof is a colossal complex: it is a housing scheme over 100-kilometre-long; a residential village containing 1800 apartments, courtyards (*Höfe*), gardens and amenities for 5,000 inhabitants; nursery school, health centre, laundries, public baths, two dozen shops, a pharmacy, a preventorium (for sufferers of tuberculosis) and even a furnishing consultant. The central block is well-known for its powerful and original appearance: it has an ochre-coloured, linear façade, as backdrop for orthogonal, russet-red volumes, intended to resemble over-sized Japanese pictograms, or gigantic anthropomorphic figures, with arched bases (splayed legs), pairs of balconies (arms), a central tower (body and head). The buildings stand side by side in a monumental sequence that elevates and characterises the scheme. The complex attracted great criticism, largely from Loos, who favoured small-scale interventions. It is now seen as being emblematic of large-scale European social housing interventions carried out in the two decades between 1920 and 1940.

Karl Ehn, view (right) and plan (below), Karl Marx Hof, 1930, Vienna

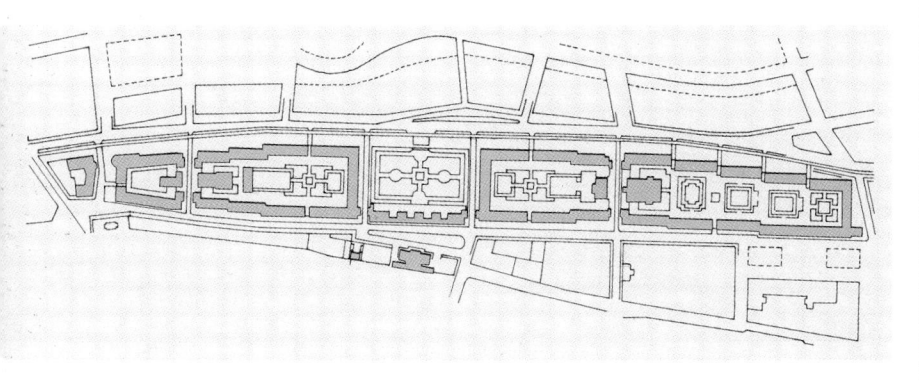

THE WERKBUND

The Austrian members of the Werkbund decided to build a low-rise prototypical housing scheme in Vienna in 1932 – an alternative kind of *'Siedlung',* or perhaps a rival scheme to the great *Höfe* under construction at that time.

Josef Frank, a pupil of Adolf Loos; not the sole Austrian, but the only member of the group to have taken part in the 1927 Stuttgart Exposition, took on leadership of the organisation. Standardisation and structural experimentation were forbidden. The aim was to design new, middle class housing models that guaranteed rational distribution and levels of comfort that would illustrate the fact that each architect could conceive of a personal version. Unlike Stuttgart, there was freedom of choice over the furnishings and there was no obligation for the units to be purely functional. Frank invited around thirty architects to take part, in particular those excluded from the Stuttgart Expo: Loos and Rietveld as well as Neutra, Breuer, Lurçat and many other Austrian architects. The site was level and the buildings were to be positioned in parallel rows with private gardens. Interesting, innovative designs were few and far between. Frank designed a villa with a deep cantilevered roof, Häring, (the only German invited to take part) designed a single-storey duplex, Lurçat designed a row of four houses with external cylindrical stairs and Rietveld designed a three-storey building including adjoining residential units. The district was well preserved and is still in use today, although at that time it generated controversy; the Left regarded it as being bourgeois whilst the Right thought it 'Zionist', as Frank was Jewish. This disagreement eventually led to the Austrian Werkbund disbanding. When the Nazis annexed Austria in 1933, Frank emigrated to Sweden.

opposite page, top
André Lurçat, Werkbund Housing Scheme, 1932, Vienna
Four minimalist, double-storey adjoining houses were designed by the French Rationalist architect, André Lurçat. This project is notable for the cylindrical stairways that project from the rear of the buildings.

opposite page, bottom
Richard Neutra, house, 1932, Vienna
The house has a roof terrace enlivened by a pergola and an external staircase; the only feature that adorns the building mass.

Werkbund Housing Scheme, Site plan, 1932, Vienna
(1–3) Hugo Häring
(4) Richard Bauer
(5) Josef Hoffmann
(6) Josef Frank
(7) Oskar Strnad
(8) Anton Brenner
(9) Karl Augustinus Bieber and Otto Niedermoser
(10) Walter Loos
(11) Eugen Wachberger
(12) Clemens Holzmeister
(13) André Lurçat
(14) Walter Sobotka
(15) Oskar Wlach
(16) Julius Jirasek
(17) Ernst A. Plischke
(18) Josef Wenzel
(19) Oswald Haerdtl
(20) Ernst Lichtblau
(21) Hugo Gorge
(22) Jacques Groag
(23) Richard Neutra
(24) Hans Adolf Vetter
(25–26) Adolf Loos
(27) Gerrit Rietveld
(28) Max Fellerer
(29) Otto Breuer
(30) Margarete Schütte-Lihotzky
(31) Arthur Grünberger
(32) Josef Franz Dex
(33) Gabriel Guévrékian
(34) Helmut Wagner-Freynsheim

THE NETHERLANDS

The ten-storey-high social housing blocks favoured by Gropius became popular in the Netherlands just a few years later during the 1930s.

Johannes Duiker (1890–1935), an underrated architect, wrote an essay along with a prototype design in 1930 espousing the advantages of building vertically and demonstrating the economic, health and functional advantages of urban expansion. This theory overrode Oud and the tenants of the Amsterdam School, which had promoted two or four-storey blocks, as well as the Delft School, which favoured country-style houses. The same stance was taken by the avant-garde Dutch journal, *De 8 en Opbouw* (8 in Construction).

Three young architects: Johannes Andreas Brinkmann (1902–1949), Leendert Cornelis van der Vlugt (1894–1936) and Willem van Tijen (1894–1974) built the Bergpolder social housing unit in Rotterdam in 1933/34. The block was ten storeys high (as propounded by Gropius), was orientated north-south for maximum sunlight, with the stairwell on the northern side and eight units planned per floor which could be accessed along a gallery. Thanks to its prefabricated steel frame and timber floors, the building was constructed very quickly. Continuous horizontal bands of balconies along one side offset the vertical height. The external staircase is enclosed in transparent glazing. The plan of the units follows Functionalist layouts, dispensing with corridors in favour of internal spatial continuity. Another experimental tall building in Rotterdam was the 1937/38 Plaslaan building.

Due to the disruption of the Second World War, only two prototypes of that era were ever built in the Netherlands.

below, left
Andreas Brinkmann, Leendert Cornelis van der Vlugt, Willem van Tijen, floor plan of a Bergpolder housing unit, 1934, Rotterdam, Netherlands
The apartment unit is strictly functional; consisting of an orthogonal rectangle containing the services: kitchen and bathroom, without a corridor. The sitting room adjoins the bedrooms; the main bedroom has double doors so that it can be integrated into the sitting room if required. The small balcony replaces the traditional Dutch external space.

Andreas Brinkmann, Leendert Cornelis van der Vlugt, Willem van Tijen, staircase detail (bottom, right) and façade (opposite page), the Bergpolder, 1934, Rotterdam, Netherlands
The development of social housing in post-1920 Central Europe culminated in a variety of different solutions. Tall residential buildings, as advocated by the likes of Gropius, Le Corbusier and Duiker were slow to take root. The Bergpolder in Rotterdam was one of the first schemes to be realised. It was ten storeys high, with eight units per floor, which could be accessed along a circulation gallery. The building was featured at the 1934 Amsterdam Exhibition on residential construction as well as at the 1937 Paris CIAM conference on the Functional City.

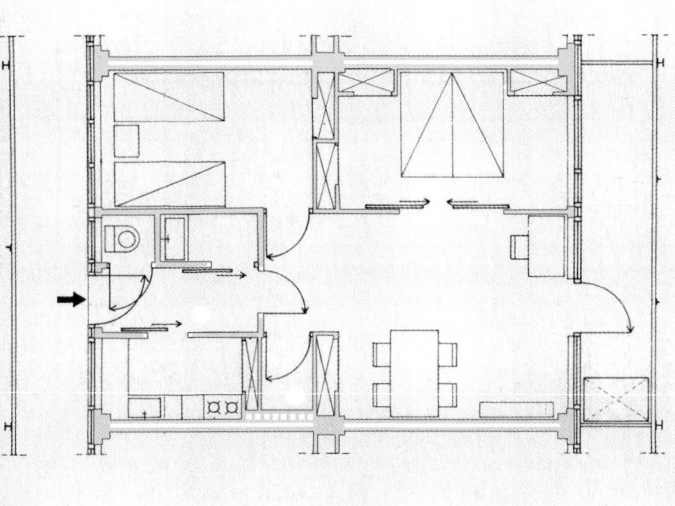

FRANCE

Between 1920 and 1940, France was the liveliest of Europe's cultural centres, witnessing a great variety of contemporary architectural movements: the plastic and formal Cubism of Hyppolyte Abraham (1891–1966) displayed in a house in Rue Jasmin, Paris (1923) that was influenced by Czech Cubisism, or the 1929 Haute Savoie sanitoria; the rational and purist Cubism of Robert Mallet Stevens in his houses in Paris (1927); the sophistication of Henri Sauvage, who built stepped terraced houses and the 1928 La Samaritaine Department Store in Paris. Other examples of the variety of work produced, included Le Corbusier's myriad of architectural works; Auguste and Gustave Perret's works in reinforced concrete, (epitomised in their 1923 Nôtre Dame du Raincy, where structural lightness is interpreted as a Gothic metaphor, with completely perforated walls); Pierre Chareau's functionalist Experimentalism, (where he replaced two entire floors of a building with a 'House of Glass' clad entirely in glass blocks, proving innovative in both layout, furnishing and lighting); the completely glazed school by Eugène Beaudoin and Marcel Lods in Suresnes (1935); the Neo-Humanism that re-evaluated the stylistic purism with a new, rational Neo-Classicism which, in turn, influenced

Pierre Chareau and Bernard Bijvoet, Glass House, detail and view, 1927–1931, Paris
This glasshouse was an astounding technical feat, achieved by demolishing two levels of a building to create a glazed block. Other innovations included the lighting, which consisted of external spotlights, the double-storey living room and the walls, which were replaced by built-in furnishings.

numerous public buildings. Examples of these projects are the Musée d'Outremer in Paris (1938) the Public Works building, the Palais de Chaillot (1938) and the town hall in Suresnes (1938). Finally, there was the Functionalism of André Lurçat who built the artists' house in Rue Seurat in Paris and later the Karl Marx College in Villejuif (1933). The residential scheme in Villeurbanne near Lyons (1934) is also noteworthy. Meanwhile, the Exposition des Arts Décoratifs et Industriels Modernes, held in Paris in 1925, kick-started the Art Deco movement. The following Exposition, held in 1937, was the fruit of lengthy debate and, under last-minute pressure from the Front Populaire, fresh from their electoral victory in 1936, show-cased the monumental Stalinist Russian and Nazi German pavilions, both of which were even awarded prizes. Picasso's famous anti-war painting, Guernica, was also shown at the Exposition, while Le Corbusier's work was relegated to a pavilion on the periphery.

ENGLAND

Between 1920 and 1940 England remained culturally cut-off: the continental avant-garde movements having failed to extend across the Channel. Vorticism, a short-lived variation on Futurism, was the only national movement (1913–1915) which conceived of shapes depicted in a vortex of movement. The British Arts and Crafts Movement as well as the Neo-Gothic architecture of George Gilbert Scott (1811–1878) continued, along with a post-Eclectic style of civic architecture that produced works such as the town halls in Cardiff and Watford.

The Modern Movement was brought into Britain by immigrants; most importantly, Berthold Lubetkin (1901–1990), a Georgian who studied in Russia and France. Lubetkin established the Tecton Studio in 1930, which produced two famous pavilions for the London Zoo: the Gorilla House and the iconic Penguin Pool. Between 1933–1935, Lubetkin designed a residential block on, at that time, the outskirts of London in Highpoint: High Point I, where he applied techniques to high-rise buildings that he had learned from Gropius, as well as principles from Le Corbusier such as roof terraces, banded windows and open-plan layouts. Wells Coates (1895–1958) built what was considered to be a very avant-garde complex in 1934 on Lawn Road in Hampstead. The building had galleries and an external staircase. Breuer, Gropius and Mondrian all lived in the building.

All three architects had fled Nazi persecution and sought refuge in England in 1933. Despite their established reputations, the three architects received few commissions; England was still a conservative environment and was diffident towards immigrants. Gropius managed to design several houses and a school while Mendelsohn won a competition to build the De La Warr seaside pavilion in Bexhill. Their lack of success in England prompted all three German architects to move to America a few years later. Few British architects were very active during that period; the most notable contribution being the Boots pharmaceutical factory in Beeston (1930–1932) by Owen Williams. The factory had mushroom-shaped concrete columns and continuous glass curtain walls.

left
Berthold Lubetkin/Tecton Studio, Highpoint I, Highgate, 1933–1935, London
This was the first building in England to be built along Rationalist principles. Constructed according to a double-cruciform plan, the building has two internal split-level elliptical staircases in the centre of each cross. It borrows from Gropius's high-rise blocks as well as from Le Corbusier's five points of architecture: pilotis elevating the building, free plan, free façade, horizontal strip windows and roof-terrace.

right
Wells Coates, Lawn Road Estate, Hampstead, 1932, London
The architect and designer, Wells Coates, designed this house in 1932. It is an orthogonal block with external galleries and stairs. It was such an innovative building for England at the time that famous artists such as Breuer, Gropius and Mondrian, chose to live there.

Berthold Lubetkin/Studio Tecton,
Penguin Pool, 1934, London
The penguin pool was Berthold
Lubetkin and the Tecton Studio's very
first commission. The curving slides
for the penguins, raised up out of the
water, were conceived as a Constructivist work, with references to the
sculpture of the artist, Gabo: like
Lubetkin, Gabo originally came from
Georgia. The bold structure was constructed from concrete with steel
supports. The structural engineer was
Ove Arup, the most renowned British
engineer.

ARCHITECTURE UNDER EUROPEAN FASCISM

Fascism took hold in Italy as early as 1922, whilst Hitler rose to power in Germany in 1933 and Stalin eventually took complete power in the Soviet Union in mid-1941. Similar totalitarian governments held their grip on power in other parts of Europe, such as Spain, Yugoslavia, Bulgaria and Romania. Dictators tended to see architecture as a fundamental means of expressing their absolute power. For these power-hungry men architecture was seen to represent solemnity, magniloquence, history, solidity and endurance. Architecture had to have its own, unequivocal and timeless language. It is perhaps unsurprising then that European dictators embraced the same kind of styles, regardless of their particular political persuasion: Neo-Classicism, Neo-Greek (Soviet Union and Germany) or Neo-Roman (Italy and France). Thus Stalinist and Nazi buildings had a great deal in common. Stalin issued a decree banning all free architects' associations and set up a state-run institution; he decreed that Neo-Greek should be the style applied to public buildings. This censorship of anything deemed 'unsoviet' was to last until 1940. Residential housing schemes were based on Neo-Realism and on the Viennese 'Hof' model. Hitler, who had aspired to be an architect as a young man, nationalised German architecture associations; he also closed schools that were avant-garde, including the Bauhaus. Hitler was in favour of Neo-Greek architecture but advocated building new, semi-rural villages as residential settlements. The avant-garde movements, inevitably anti-historic and ephemeral by nature, were also provocative and revolutionary in character. The avant-garde movements were established by a few like-minded people; they were seen as a threat to the establishment and so were naturally outlawed. The public buildings that were commissioned followed the same dictates and a great many classical statues and large paintings or mosaics depicted subjects that symbolised and glorified the repressive regimes. The vast majority of architects (those who had not fled) were almost unanimously compliant; although just how much conviction they really had will never be known.

Marcello Piacentini, Palazzo del
Rettorato, La Sapienza University,
1932–1935, Rome

ARCHITECTURE IN ITALY

The architectural scene in Italy between 1920 and 1940 was unusual and rather different from the rest of Europe. Italy was the only country with a dictatorial regime that lasted throughout both decades; its political rise to power in 1922 came several years before contemporary architectural movements discovered their own identities. While the regime was taking root (1922–1928), figurative proponents and militant critics were calling for a "return to order" in order to avert a revival of eclectic or floral designs, or indeed any of the pre-war figurative avant-garde styles. The first signs of renewal in the world of fine art was the publication of *La Ronda* (1919), a magazine featuring works by de Chirico, Carrà, Campigli, Sironi, as well as by the sculptors, Marini and Martini. This was followed by another review, *Valori Plastici*. The publication of these magazines laid the foundations for the Novecento Movement — its name suggesting that it was representative of the 20th century. This movement also encompassed architects: Giovanni Muzio (1893–1982), Gio Ponti (1891–1979), Ottavio Cabiati (1889–1956) and others. The Novecento Movement reworked Metaphysical depictions through the simplified formal principles of the Secession, employing Classical and geometric references in monumental buildings. The so-called 'Ca' Bruta' building by Muzio (1923) was symbolic of the movement, launching a new architectural language with a compact, curvilinear building. The axial sym-

Giovanni Muzio, Ca' Bruta, 1923, Milan
Both the general public and critics were horrified by Muzio's first major work, Ca' Bruta. They were shocked by the composition of the volume, the curved façade with its axial symmetry, the scale of the building and the variety of geometric decorative elements – partly Classical and partly invented. It was an innovative project that deviated strongly from the traditional canons; the local Milanese were highly critical of it, dubbing it Ca'Bruta (ugly building).

metry of the building was lateral rather than central and featured a large arch and superficial ornamentation consisting of tympanums, latticework, alcoves, niches and cornices. The architectural vocabulary was gleaned from many other architectural sources, Milan in particular, with the delicate colour-palette of its buildings such as the hues favoured by Luigi Gigiotti Zanini (1893–1962), who was also a painter, and the sophisticated, volumetric and decorative compositions of Gio Ponti, or the more sombre style of Giuseppe de Finetti (1892–1952), who had studied in Vienna. For several years this group of architects worked in adjacent studios to another of the movement's exponents, Alberto Alpago Novello (1889–1985).

The Novecento Movement built palaces and villas for the bourgeoisie; commissions that were often critically received.

In 1926, a group of young architects in Milan set up the Gruppo 7. These architects included: Luigi Figini, Guido Frette, Sebastiano Larco, Ubaldo Castagnoli, later to be replaced by Adalberto Libera, Gino Pollini, Carlo Enrico Rava and Giuseppe Terragni. Gruppo 7 represented European Rationalism and was eager to stress that it was not anti-historic, but rather a mouthpiece for the spirit of the times; and therefore represented Fascist artists. This was the only group to have any international links (some of them even took part in CIAM meetings). They adhered to the same codes as the Modern Movement: volumetric rigour, formal minimalism, functionality and absence of colour.

The most representative works were the House Figini (1903–1984) in Milan, which was based on Corbusian principles (pilotis, open plan, roof garden) and those of Terragni (1904–1943). Terragni, who came from Como, designed only few truly typical buildings, but those that did exemplify Rationalist canons include Novocomum (1927–1929), a residence with clear references to Russian Constructivism, four houses in Milan and the Casa del Fascio in Como (1932–1936), which is one of the most representative Rationalist buildings.

During the same period, Marcello Piacentini (1881–1960), who had also been influenced by Milanese Novecento, was given numerous public commissions. He was trying to develop a simplified monumental style with eclectic influences, yet with no concessions to the new Neo-Classicism of the Fascist regimes. Regarded in hindsight, the three contemporaneous movements were clearly all seeking a 'return to order' despite their different approaches.

In 1926 Mussolini delivered a famous speech in Perugia, in which he declared that Fascism did not want a 'regime style of art'. Although the preferred, but not exclusive, aesthetic for public buildings during the Fascist era was Monumentalism, acknowledgment was also sought elsewhere, such as in the restoration and enclosure of great Roman monuments (such as the Imperial Forum) and the demolition of some historical city centres to make way for new, wide boulevards and piazzas celebrating Fascism. The creation of new cities and building projects in the colonies were also priorities.

Together with the gallery owner, Pietro Maria Bardi (1900–1999), Marcello Piacentini played a seminal role in the interaction between the various movements. Piacentini, the Fascist regime's de facto architect, always took a central, role mediating between the groups, managing and allocating commissions, tenders and procurements. Bardi, an advisor to Mussolini, championed Rationalism as a young, revolutionary and therefore, Fascist art form. He published a report on architecture for Mussolini in 1931.

The first obvious consequence of Bardi's report was the freedom of exhibitions. A professional institute for the 'industrial arts' was set up in Monza in 1922, which set up the first Biennial Exposition of Decorative Arts a year later, showcasing Novecento works. After four events, it evolved into the Milan Triennale (1933), becoming the leading architectural, pictorial and decorative arts event in Italy. The Biennial became increasingly geared to Rationalist architecture; the first exhibition focusing on Rationalist architecture was held in Rome in 1928. The MIAR (Italian Movement for Rational Architecture) managed to recruit architects from all over Italy. The first major architectural reviews were also launched in 1928: *La Casa Bella,* edited by Giuseppe Pagano (1896–1945) and Edoardo Persico (1900–1936) and *Domus,* edited by Gio Ponti.

This was an intense period of activity for the government as far as public building projects was concerned. The party needed Fascist headquarters for the Italian Fascist Youth Organisation, it also needed stadiums as well as other public buildings: railway stations and post offices in particular, even buildings for their colonies. The groups collaborated on the Exhibition of the Fascist Revolution in Rome in 1932 to celebrate the tenth anniversary of its rise to power. Libera and De Rienzi designed the entrance, whilst Terragni and Nizzoli as well as the artists,

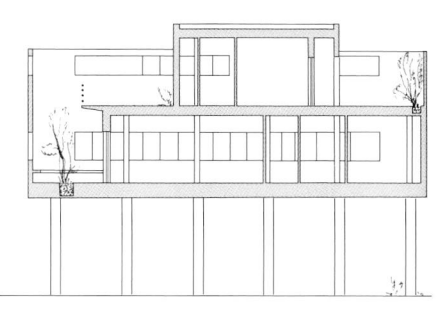

Luigi Figini, section of his own house, 1935, Milan
This small building was designed along international Rationalist principles and Corbusian planning criteria. It is a bold, orthogonal, white box supported by slender pilotis. The interior is open-plan. The roof has a terrace held within parapet walls.

opposite page
Marcello Piacentini, Piazza della Vittoria, 1928–1932, Brescia
The ideology of fascism was represented in boulevards and monumental squares, modelled on the glory days of Imperial Rome and the idealised vision of the Renaissance. Fascism left its indelible mark on some of the leading historic city centres, which were decimated in order to make way for new thoroughfares, such as Via della Conciliazione in Rome and the Via Roma in Turin as well as city squares like the Piazza della Vittoria in Brescia. Piacentini built piazzas based on what was regarded as an ideal model: a rectangular layout, surrounded by monumental buildings with porticoes, a civic tower and axial access streets.

Sironi and Funi Prampolini collaborated along with the writer, Leo Longanesi, who set up the Mussolini Room. Libera was also commissioned to build the Italian pavilions in expos held in Chicago (1933) and Brussels (1935).

Piacentini designed the masterplan for Rome University campus in 1932, commissioning various architects such as Giuseppe Pagano, Gio Ponti, Arnaldo Foschini and Giovanni Michelucci from Florence, as well as several younger architects. The most significant buildings of the period were the Post Office in Rome (1935) by Mario Ridolfi and Mario Fagiolo and the central Post Office in Naples (1936) by Giuseppe Vaccaro. Both were elongated, austere buildings: the post office in Rome had a strong, curved short elevation whilst the post office in Naples had a over-scaled entrance. The competition to build the railway station in Florence (1934) was awarded to a group led by Giovanni Michelucci (1891–1990). Their design displayed a blend of tradition as well as technical and formal innovation. The Fascist regime was also involved in three main aspects of town planning: demolishing historic city centres in order to create new boulevards such as Via della Conciliazione in Rome and Via Po in Turin as well as monumental piazzas like Piazza della Vittoria in Brescia; creating new districts within Italy and in its colonies; creating urban plans for numerous cities such as, for example: Arezzo, Bolzano, Pavia, Como and Aosta. This led to the first town planning conference being held in 1937 and to the subsequent issuing of national town planning legislation in 1942. Other architects in Italy began to make their mark with important works in the late 1930s: Ignazio Gardella (1905–1999) with the anti-tuberculosis dispensary in Alessandria (1938) and Carlo Mollino (1905–1973), who designed a riding school in Turin (1940); these works were Rationalist with historic references.

left
Adalberto Libera and Mario de Renzi, façade of the Exhibition of the Fascist Revolution at the Palazzo delle Esposizioni, 1932, Rome
A Rationalist scheme by Libera was selected for this eclectic façade. The building consisted of a colossal 30-metre-high cube. The façade featured four projecting oval tubes, 2.5 metres wide and 25 metres high, with 6-metre-high axes, on a slender roof forty metres long and cantilevered four metres, a complex that was converted for several subsequent exhibitions.

right
Luigi Moretti, exterior view and interior view of the Accademia di Scherma, 1933–1936, Rome
Moretti's designs were at times Rational and at other times structurally bold, but were always very innovative. This fencing pavilion, one of several sports buildings, is a masterpiece of austerity: it sits above a stepped base, with fenestration on the lower section beneath a solid stone-faced upper volume. Fissures in the roof allow for natural light.

In 1938 a group of Milanese architects came up with the concept for the Città del Sole, a large, strictly Rationalist district (never built) which featured identical tower blocks distributed in parallel rows, all orientated in the same direction. However, the group did also build the more modest Filzi district, with ten parallel buildings of varying heights. In 1941, Piacentini started to plan the 1942 EUR (Universal Exposition in Rome), to coincide with the twentieth anniversary of Fascism. After initial disagreements — especially with Pagano, who rejected the concept of the 'Monumentalisation of empty space' — architects from various groups decided to take part. However, the War thwarted the exposition, which was to have consisted of a new district with residential and commercial components. A few monumental institutional buildings have survived from that era, for instance the magnificent Palazzo della Civiltà Italiana.

Adalberto Libera, Palazzo dei Congressi, 1938–1942, Rome
Libera designed this palazzo to be monumentally classical, centrally symmetrical and horizontally arranged. It has a long extended colonnade of cylindrical columns supporting a slender vault.

THE MASTERPIECE
CASA DEL FASCIO/FASCIST HEADQUARTERS

By 1933, Stalin had banned all avant-garde movements; whilst Hitler had risen to power, forcing the Bauhaus to close and all its best teachers to flee the country. Thus the choice of Giuseppe Terragni – the most representative of all Italian Rationalist architects – to build the Casa del Fascio in Como was rather surprising. Terragni's design for the Fascist Headquarters was utterly radical: it consisted of a beautifully proportioned volume devoid of any projections, built to a square plan. The façades face the four cardinal points, the most historically traditional orientation. The orthogonal structure is open on two elevations; the front elevation of the building consists of a four-storey grid containing seven horizontal modules, five of

them open and two clad in concrete, to create an asymmetrical composition. The building is monochrome; the entire building painted white. The first lofty double-volume entrance lobby, the two upper levels are U-shaped, with a central courtyard; many of the walls are constructed with glass tiles, set in a tight structural grid, reminiscent of Charles Rennie Mackintosh and Josef Hoffmann's Art Nouveau designs. The Casa del Fascio was built as a totalitarian building, a manifesto for Italian Rationalism, with clear references to the geometric designs of the local Como School of abstract art (with exponents such as Aldo Galli, Mario Radice and Manlio Rho), orientated towards the historic city centre and the apse of the Duomo.

Giuseppe Terragni, façade of the Casa del Fascio, 1932–1936, Como
The Casa del Fascio was by no means the most representative of all European Rationalist buildings. It diverted from the principles of Rationalism in a variety of ways: the extreme austerity of its Cartesian structural grid, the fact that its dimensions were calculated according to the golden ratio, the square floor plan, a pure and absolute shape, as well as the atrium, piers and concrete-framed glass blocks.

Giuseppe Terragni, ground floor
entrance lobby, Casa del Fascio, 1933,
Como

FASCIST URBAN PLANNING: THE NEW CITIES

Planning a new city in Italy was inevitably rooted in history, particularly Roman history. The Fascists seized the opportunity to plan settlements with a blend of functionality and urban planning which they used as propaganda. The town, Guidonia in Lazio was built for the aeronautics industry, Carbonia was built for miners, Fertilia for farmers in Sardinia and Segezia for local peasants in Apulia. New cities were also constructed in Italian colonies; particularly in Somalia. The major event in Italy was the reclamation of Agro Pontino (Pontine Marshes), the largest malaria infested swamp area in the country, which had the advantage of being close to the capital. Under Mussolini's motto 'land for the peasants', land was given to (forced) migrants from the Veneto and the Marshes. During the five year period between 1932 and 1937, many cities were built, such as Littoria (now Latina), Sabaudia, Pontinia, Aprilia and Pomezia, with evocative names like 'honouring the Savoia family', 'lictorial fasces', 'Pontine Marshes', 'the month in which they were founded', 'the fruit they produced'. Commissions were awarded according to various procedures: direct commissions, such as Oriolo Frezzotti's (1888–1965) commission for Littoria; competitions, such as the one won by Gino Cancellotti's (1896–1967) team for Sabaudia and Concezio Petrucci's (1902–1946) for Aprilia and Pomezia; or else as part of official commissions, as in Pontinia. The schemes had to be 'rural and longitudinal' (Piacentini). In the rest of Europe new cities were not being developed; although housing settlements followed the same layout as German '*Siedlungen*', (parallel rows of housing blocks), the novelty lay in the urban centres, which consisted of a traditional Italian piazza, with a church, town hall, post office and high street with continuous façades. Latina is built to a concentric, radial plan and Pomezio has an elongated plan, sited on a north: south orientation. The houses were simple country homes; however buildings of importance were also built, such as the public buildings in the town, Sabaudia, designed by Eugenio Montuori, Luigi Piccinato, Gino Cancellotti, Alfredo Scalpelli and Angiolo Mazzoni which included the railway station and the post office building in Latina and the post office in Sabaudia.

opposite page
View of the main piazza in Aprilia, 1936, Latina
A view from a street through an arch that frames the bell-tower, a distinctive feature of all the new Fascist cities.

Piazza in Sabaudia, 1934, Latina
Sabaudia is the most noteworthy new Fascist city: urban planning criteria dictated that there had to be a central piazza on a rectangular plan, according to Italian tradition, with a town hall and a church. The lictorial tower was used as a Fascist device, a reworking of medieval towers, symbolic of all cities.

GERMANY

Hitler was an architect manqué, culturally rooted in Eclecticism. When the despot seized power in 1933, he believed that architecture had a scenographic, symbolic and didactic part to play in two different spheres: state architecture had to be monumental and impressive, while local architecture had to conform to local tradition. Modernist architecture was thought to be oriental in origin – possibly even Bolshevik – and could not be reconciled with his vision of what architecture ought to be. The Bauhaus was forced to close and all modernist architects who had been practising the discipline in Germany were forced to emigrate. Mies van der Rohe, who had already made some experimental forays into Modernism, was the only avant-garde architect left in Germany by 1938. He took part in various design competitions without success. Official Nazi architecture had to be Neo-Classical, Neo-Greek at best, but certainly grandiose and colossal. The first architect to be commissioned by the dictatorial regime was Paul Ludwig Troost (1878–1934), who built the German Art Museum in Munich (1933–1937). The long, elongated front elevation of the museum was adorned with a simplified Doric portico in a reinterpretation of the great Neo-Classical buildings in Munich. Troost was succeeded by the infamous Albert Speer (1905–1981), who designed the imposing backdrops for the huge ceremonial propaganda events held by the Nazis that were framed by monumental colonnades like stage sets, such as the one for the 1934 Nuremburg Rally. Speer was convinced that his fascist buildings would be seen as 'valuable ruins' several hundred years hence. In 1936 Hitler managed to win the commission to host the Olympic Games, which would transform Berlin into the 'new Athens'. Hitler had the massive stadium built by the architect, Werner March. The following year, in 1937, Speer designed the German pavilion at the Paris Exposition; an imposing, sinister tower facing the Soviet pavilion, surmounted by an eagle and a swastika. It would appear that Speer had been able to see the design of the Russian pavilion by the architect, Iofan, well before the expo, thus enabling him to design a building of similar grand proportions. During this period Hitler and Speer were also working on an urban plan for Berlin: conceived on a 5-kilometre-long central radius between an arch and an enormous 200-metre-high skyscraper adorned with a cupola. The Second World War put a halt to their plans; bombing systematically destroyed Nazi buildings in Berlin — the 1935 House of Ministers was one of the only Nazi building that escaped serious damage.

opposite page, top
Paul Ludwig Troost, German Art Museum, 1933, Munich, Germany
Prior to his premature death in 1934, Troost had been Hitler's favoured architect due to the Classical style of his designs, in stark contrast to the architecture of the Jugendstil. The museum is a simple building, with a monumental Doric colonnade. The building is a classical evocation and reinterpretation of the role of the city that had once been a capital of Neo-Classicism.

opposite page, bottom
Albert Speer, viewing stands at the Zeppelinfeld rally, 1935–1937, Nuremburg, Germany
This stand is the most imposing of Albert Speer's projects. It was a kind of theatrical backdrop, which consisted of an over-scaled Neo-Greek colonnade with a simplified design that had amplified dimensions. Speer was a personal acquaintance of Hitler and Minister of Armaments.

Albert Speer, German Pavilion, 1937, Paris, France
Germany had produced sensational pavilions for both the Paris Expo of 1925 and the Barcelona Expo of 1929. Speer designed a simplified Classical tower with pilasters on opposite façades and adorned with a cornice. The project was rushed through in order to be able to compete with the Soviet pavilion in terms of height and symbolic content: the eagle and swastika at the apex, directly vis à vis the enormous iconic statue of the Soviet workman and peasant.

THE SOVIET UNION

Stalin gradually managed to gain absolute power between 1928 and 1933 (with the expulsion of Trotsky and other internal opponents). The despot then decreed that all artistic and architectural activities had to be in the service of the state; he dissolved all cultural associations and set up state watchdogs. Soviet art was used as a medium of state propaganda; it had to be eloquent and communicate directly to the populace though hyper-realistic paintings, statues and painting, all executed on a monumental scale in order to honour the most powerful proletarian state in the world.

Efforts were concentrated on the capital, Moscow: the new regulatory plan (1932–1935) was strictly radial. Old districts were gutted to make way for new monumental streets, working class districts were constructed and there were plans for a twenty-kilometre-long boulevard with numerous public squares and public buildings (which were never built).

The first underground stations opened between 1933 and 1940. They had to be monumental stations, unrivalled anywhere in the world, similar to the reception rooms in luxurious palaces or art galleries: these were the magnificent spaces for the people, designed in a heady blend of New-Baroque and Socialist Realism.

The competition to build the Palace of the Soviets evolved in four stages between 1930 and 1934. The architects invited to take part included Le Corbusier, Mendelsohn, Perret and Poelzig. The competition was won by Boris Iofan (1891–1976), who designed a 400-metre-high tower, with a colonnade at its base, containing a Soviet hall with a cupola crowned with a massive fluted column, a pedestal for a statue of Lenin approximately 75-metres-high. Construction began in 1937 —

Boris Iofan, design for the Palace of the Soviets, 1930–1934
The skyscraper was designed to be approximately 400 metres tall, in order to rival the Empire State Building in New York, shaped like the shaft of a column and crowned with a statue of Lenin, 75-metres-high. This project won the competition not only as it was monumental, imposing and evocative, but also as it contained all the necessary references to the Neo-Greek culture that was *de rigueur* at the time. Because of the prevailing anti-religious, atheist climate, the construction was to have been built on the site of the church of Christ the Saviour, which had been blown up with dynamite. Construction began in 1937 but was cut short by the War, never to be resumed.

Boris Iofan, Soviet Pavilion, 1937, Paris
This imposing pavilion strengthened ties between the Soviet Union and France, which had been governed by the Social Communist Popular Front from 1936. It was an impressive stepped structure adorned with an enormous statue of the iconic *Peasant and Worker*.

regarded as the harshest year of Stalinist repression — on the former site of the church of Christ the Saviour, which was demolished during the obligatory period of atheism, but was put to a halt by the War in 1940, never to be resumed.

The discipline of architecture was placed entirely in the hands of academics like, Aleksej Schusev, Lev Rudnev and Boris Iofan. Stalin commissioned Iofan to design the Soviet pavilion at the 1937 Paris Exposition. He designed a stepped monument, crowned by *Vera Ignat'evna* Muchin's sculpture of the worker and peasant, set confidently opposite a Nazi icon on the German pavilion. Two years later Iofan was also commissioned to design the pavilion for the New York Exposition. The War called a halt to Stalin's schemes, which were resumed in 1950 with the building of the several Neo-Gothic high-risers in Moscow.

FINAL TRENDS OF THE 1930S

There were numerous cultural movements that sprang up on the international architectural scene after 1930. The most important breakthrough came with Alvar Aalto, who lived in Finland, a country apparently far-removed from the new trends. After a brief Romantic, Neo-Classical period, Aalto developed a new blend of the widespread Rationalist vocabulary — as in Viipuri Library — and a spatial and material fusion with nature, inspired by his homeland. Aalto's organic architecture sought to achieve a harmonious balance between the built and natural environments, either enveloping space or being enveloped by it. He designed triangular, sinuous, fan-shaped shapes (as in the Paimio Sanatorium) using simple materials — plaster, brick and timber — sometimes detailed in craftsman-like fashion (Villa Mairea at Noormarku), in an aesthetic that was to become widely popular after the war. This development was followed by the German Organic Movement, which laid the foundations for Hans Scharoun's work in Berlin.

Other significant architectural developments included design engineering, which produced some fine buildings in reinforced concrete (a material that offered new technical possibilities), structures like stadiums, bridges and hangars of great aesthetic and formal quality were also built. Furthermore, there was the German Liturgical Movement, which produced dozens of churches based on in-depth research into the altar: congregation: choir ratio as well as the new vogue for English gardens based on chromatic floral research. These were all currents that, although circumscribed and short-lived, had a significant influence on the post-war architectural scene.

Alvar Aalto, Villa Mairea, 1939,
Noormarkku, Finland

LE CORBUSIER: GRAND DESIGNS 1930–1940

Le Corbusier was not only an architect, he was also a painter and a designer of sculptures (executed for him by craftsmen) as well as a theorist, writer, polemicist and a great orator and communicator, quite unlike any of his contemporaries. He also organised exhibitions and conferences. He was so totally dedicated to his work, that he seemed to renounce his private life.

Le Corbusier already enjoyed international fame by the late 1920s and undertook some incredible projects over the following decade. Thanks to a Soviet Minister with a passion for architecture, he was commissioned to build the Centosoyuz in Moscow (1928–1935); an office building for 3,500 staff as well as a theatre. He also built the Salvation Army Hostel in Paris (1925–1932) and he designed the Swiss Pavilion (Switzerland was his native country) at the university campus in Paris.

In 1932 Le Corbusier built a residential block with rooms on two floors (duplexes) in Geneva, named Maison Clarté (House of Light) due to its glass curtain walls and the use of glass blocks held within concrete frames. At last Le Corbusier was able to showcase the Immeuble-villas he had designed a decade earlier in 1922. These were double-storey blocks, each with their own roof terrace, arranged in two volumes around an internal garden. It was a model that had been previously employed in a spirit of propaganda for the Esprit Nouveau Pavilion at the 1925 Paris Exposition (reconstructed for the SAIE Trade Fair in Bologna). Le Corbusier was also invited to take part in two major international competitions: the first for the Palais des Nations in Geneva (1927) and the second for the Palace of the Soviets in Moscow (1931). Le Corbusier incorporated his famous 'Five Points' in both his designs, introducing alternating façades constructed entirely of glass with sections of opaque solid planes. He also incorporated innovative ventilation systems.

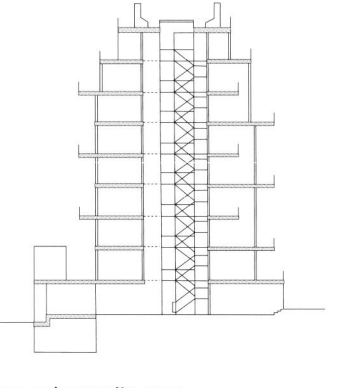

top and opposite page
Le Corbusier, section and atrium of the Maison Clarté, 1932, Geneva
Le Corbusier was perfecting an apartment typology that had double-height glazed entry spaces with balconies overlooked by bedrooms on mezzanine levels. He made abundant use of concrete-framed glass blocks in the stairwells and atrium. The internal stairwells would have been poorly lit if they were not built with transparent materials.

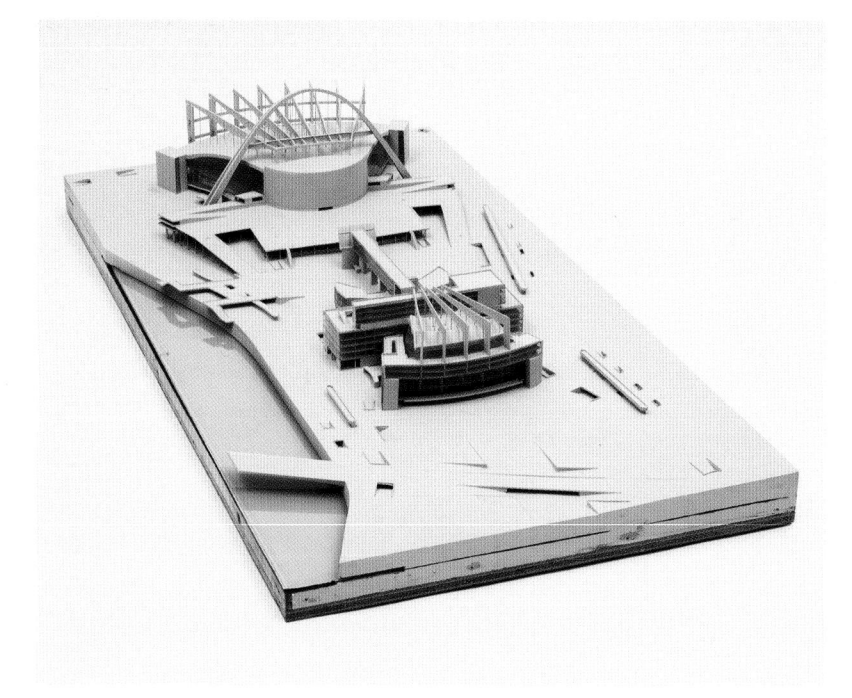

Le Corbusier, model for the Palace of the Soviets competition, 1931, Moscow
This was a complex design, consisting of two halls of different sizes on a curved plan. The design featured a large monumental arch for the Communist regime, but was unsuccessful as more conservative design was chosen that was never actually realised.

The buildings were designed to be enormous, horizontally elongated structures, accented with free-form secondary elements deriving from Le Corbusier's artistic repertoire. Examples are: the auditorium in Moscow, the stairwell in the Swiss Pavilion ("The best curved wall in modern architecture," according to the critic Siegfried Giedion) and the upper floors of the Salvation Army Hostel, where he introduced primary colours and his first floor-to-ceiling murals. Le Corbusier's entry for the Moscow competition proved that he was also an extraordinary inventor of shapes and manipulator of volumes (imitated time and again, to this day).

THE MASTERPIECE
THE SWISS PAVILION

After Le Corbusier's lack of success in the competition for the Palais des Nations in Geneva, he was awarded the commission to build the Swiss students' residence in Paris from a committee of university professors in 1930. Disheartened over his failure in the Geneva competition, he initially turned down the commission, subsequently deciding to accept it after all. The design was based on the new architectural principles that Le Corbusier had laid down three years earlier: the building was raised on pilotis, the southern curtain wall was constructed entirely of glass, the roof had a terrace and solarium within its parapet walls. The plan layout was extremely simple, consisting of three levels with a long corridor leading to a series of rooms. The spaces acted as the module for the steel structure. The opaque walls were stone-clad. The atrium and staircase are situated outside the envelope of the main block, thus juxtaposing the sinuous shapes of the piers, the curvilinear staircase and the large, sweeping blank wall in the stairwell — deriving from Le Corbusier's experience as a purist painter and sculptor — with the geometric, austere primary structure. The Rationalist vocabulary was rejected in Paris. Compared with the other international halls of residence, which were all built in a national style, the Swiss Pavilion did not in any way resemble Swiss traditional architecture and was thus heavily slated by both the public and the press in Switzerland. Despite all this, the Swiss Pavilion holds an important place in architectural history as the first large-scale work to be executed by Le Corbusier and as a seminal piece of contemporary architecture.

left
Le Corbusier, ground floor plan, Swiss Pavilion, 1930–1932, Paris
The Swiss Pavilion represented one of Le Corbusier's preferred layouts of the period: a perfectly rectangular building, elevated on pilotis with only the atrium at ground level.

Le Corbusier, Swiss Pavilion, façade (opposite page) and rear wall with external stairwell (below), 1930–1932, Paris
This image shows the open-plan ground floor, the rectangular grid of rooms, glazed walls and roof terrace with the concrete wall punctured with apertures.

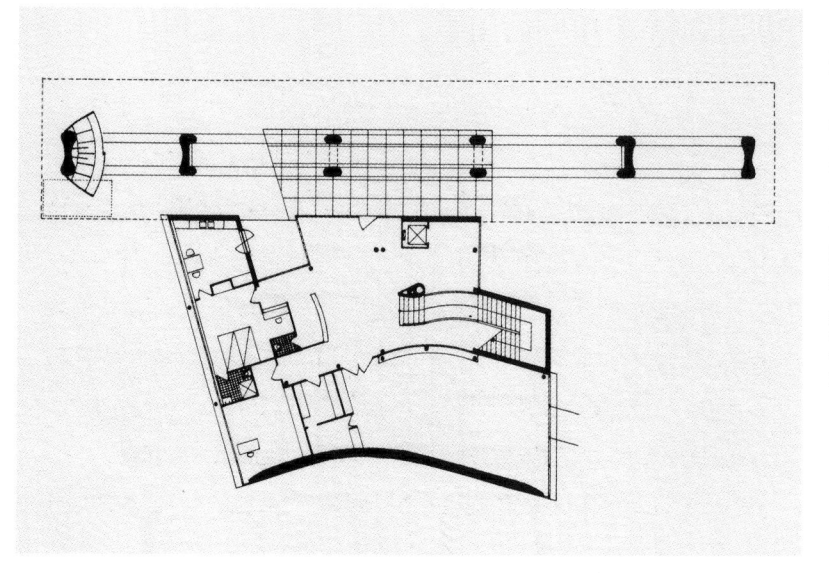

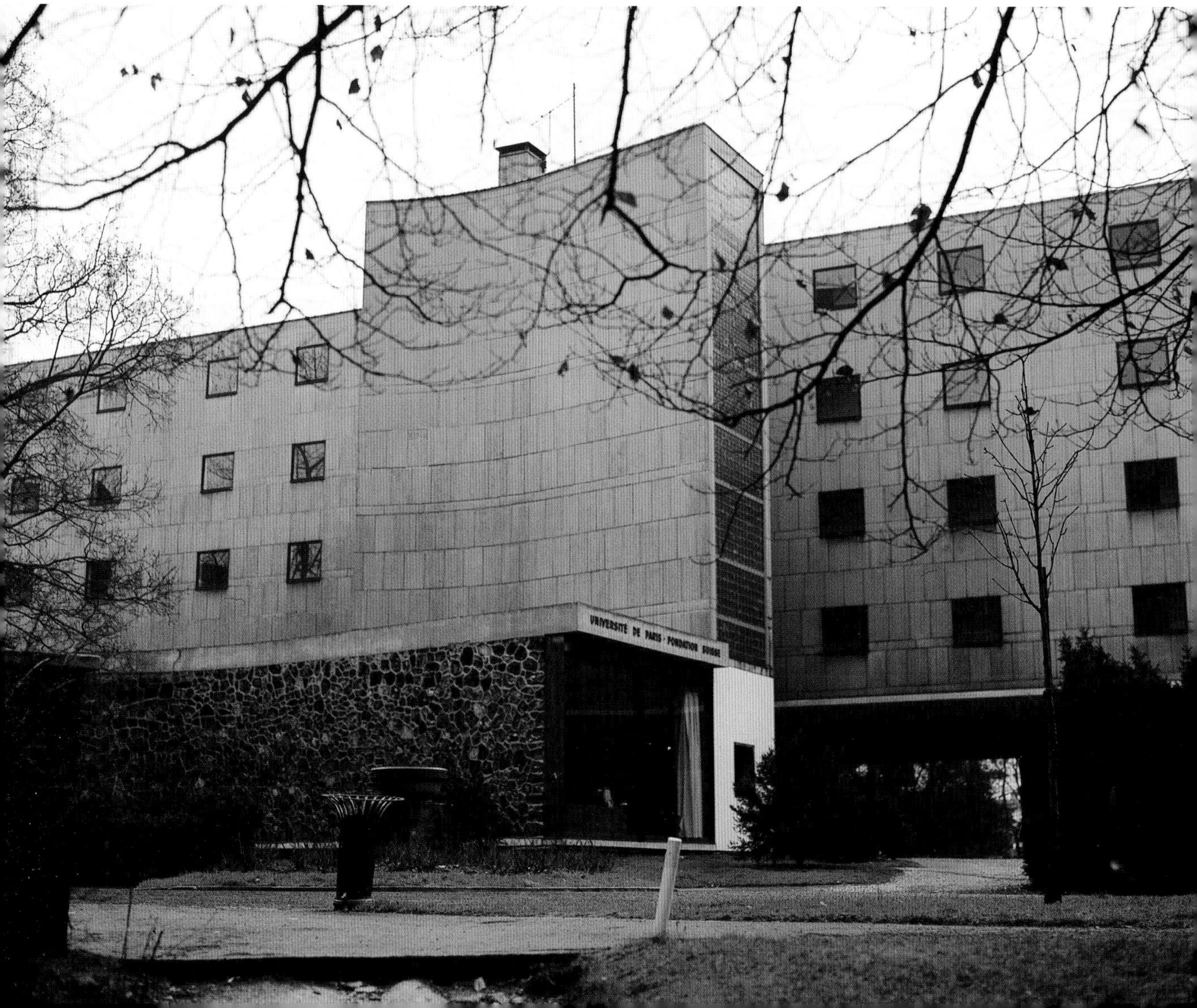

ALVAR AALTO: THE EARLY YEARS

Finland, far removed and isolated from Continental Europe, had its own architectural development, characterised by Nationalist Romanticism between the late 19th century and early 20th century. Alvar Aalto (1898–1976) was born into this era and, after starting his career in a Classical manner, began to develop an extraordinary talent for creating organic, highly original shapes, drawn from the crafts tradition. Aalto reinterpreted the Rationalist Movement in his own particular style, however he left no published theoretical texts. Aalto's sanatorium in Paimio (1929–1933) epitomises the organic Modern Movement interpretation of architecture. Its volumes are differentiated according to their function; they are composed in a fan shape, open to the sun and the trees. In 1931 Aalto designed a small building for the Toppila Paper Mill with extremely high, pitched roofs and deep overhangs; a device of his own invention that he was to use again in other factory buildings. The library in Viipuri (now Vyborg, 1935) consists of several clear volumes: the reading room is naturally lit from above and the auditorium has an undulating timber ceiling. The use of timber also characterised the Finnish Pavilions at the 1937 Paris Expo, and the 1939 New York Expo in particular, where it was

Alvar Aalto, reading room at the Vyborg Library (below, left) and undulating ceiling in the auditorium (below, right), 1935, Viipuri (now Vyborg), Russia
The reading room is the focal point of the library, naturally lit from skylights in the roof; the space continues on two levels and is connected by the fluid double stairway.
The ceiling in the conference room is an undulating wave of timber strips which enhance the acoustics, although its aesthetic value overrides its functionality. The space is enlivened by the articulation of the ceiling, a device that Aalto first used in the Finnish pavilion in New York and was subsequently to employ frequently in his buildings.

used extensively. The 1939 pavilion had an elongated wall clad with vertical timber battens, creating the impression of an undulating wave. It embodied Aalto's slow spatial dynamic, obtained with simple methods of his own invention, worked on a large-scale with the attention to detail of a cabinet-maker.

Aalto also brought all these aspects to his 1939 Villa Mairea at Noormarkku which he treated as an experimental house. The villa is built according to an L-shaped plan around a garden, which opens onto a forest. It has a free-form cantilevered roofs and special touches like the timber strips on the stairs, the projecting windows which ensure maximum light and the combined use of plaster, metal and wood on the façade. By the time he was forty years old, Aalto was already a master of architecture, a poet of material and space and a sophisticated interpreter of place and movement. These early projects laid the foundation for his later work.

Alvar Aalto, detail of the cantilevered roof and windows at Villa Mairea, 1939, Noormarkku, Finland
Allowed to work autonomously, Aalto was able to deepen the scope of his research. The overhanging eaves are extremely slender and are supported by timber columns, a device that he had previously employed in the Finnish Pavilion in Paris a few years previously. Aalto employed timber and steel in the building. Each component part of the villa is informed by research and invention, like the angled projecting windows which are positioned in order to gain maximum light and an unencumbered view of the woods.

THE MASTERPIECE
THE PAIMIO SANATORIUM

Aalto won the competition to build the Sanatorium in Paimio (1929–1933). The six-storey building has an elongated arm that runs like a spine along a forest in southern Finland. The primary 'spine' has several linked blocks attached to it, each with its own function — in-patient spaces, sitting rooms and communal spaces — all orientated different directions. This was Aalto's 'organic' design: an edifice surrounded by open landscape, flexibly conceived to suit the topography of the site, with no preconceived design, as if incorporating nature into the various volumes. This was the first example of the sinuous, undulating forms that his subsequent buildings were to adopt, a fluid interpenetration of internal and external spaces. The blocks were planned to have optimal orientation and maximum use of sunlight. For therapeutic reasons, patients were accommodated in wards which were warmed by the greenhouse effect of the glazed walls. The inhabitants followed the sun by moving from building to building during the course of the day. The primary volume was built according to a tree-shaped structure, with central 'trunks' supporting the projecting slabs, thus doing away with the need for structural columns on the curtain walls and enabling the use of continuous bands of windows. The vocabulary is Rationalist, though used in a great variety of combinations: from opaque walls to completely glazed walls, from banded windows to projecting balconies. All the fitted furnishings and detailing, from the bedrooms to the staircases, were designed by Aalto himself.

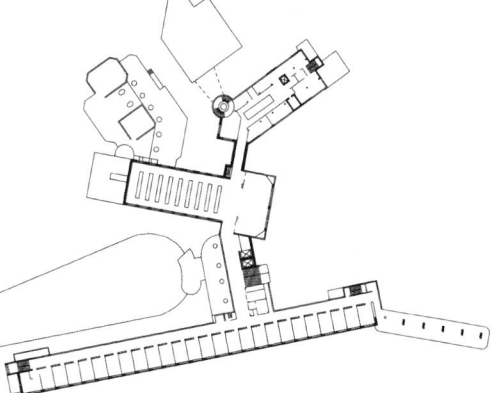

Alvar Aalto, view and plan of the Sanatorium, 1929–1933, Paimio, Finland
The sanatorium buildings are surrounded by woodlands; its pavilion blocks are orientated in different directions in order to capture solar radiation.

Alvar Aalto, detail of the ends of the
Sanatorium buildings with balconies,
1929–1933, Paimio, Finland
The patients' wards were conceived
to maximise the greenhouse effect
and are orientated out towards the
landscape.

THE ORGANIC MOVEMENT IN GERMANY

In Germany, where the most rigorous Rationalist ideals were to be found, another interpretation of architecture was springing up which was informed by Expressionism and which contained organic elements. The movement was championed by Hugo Häring (1882–1958) and Hans Scharoun (1893–1972). Häring, who was an engineer and a writer, had shared a studio with Mies van der Rohe in the late 1920s, creating the catalyst for the Der Ring group, to which many young architects belonged during that period. Häring believed that designs should not derive from preconceived and unshakeable tenets, but should rather be inspired by the environment and the needs of their users, to avoid being sterile or characterless. He also believed buildings should be made from local materials. While social housing projects in Berlin were adjusting to Rationalism, Häring was busy developing his initial ideas regarding single-family housing. The prototypical Gut Garkau Farm in Lubecca (1924–1926) has rounded masonry shapes clad with timber. Häring's friend, Hans Scharoun, a water-colourist whose Expressionist designs were inspired by Mendelsohn, showed great creative talent and managed to win several competitions during the 1920s. Scharoun also participated in schemes for large residential districts, introducing unusual curved elements, as in the Weissenhof Villa. His architecture was at its most liberated and expressive in some of his villas. Villa Schminke in Löbau (1930–1933) particularly exemplified this spirit. His treatment of the end of the villa, where he contoured the slabs to organically define wide balconies and cantilevers, independently of the receding glazed curtain walls. The villa served as a prototype for Häring's post-war architecture.

Hugo Häring, Gut Garkau Farm, 1924–1926, Klingberg, Germany
Designing farm buildings was an unusual commission, but this project dovetailed with Häring's principles and gave him the opportunity to express his poetry.
Häring designed forms that accommodated the daily activities of the farmworkers. The building has an interesting roofline and is constructed with materials that were commonly used in that part of rural Germany.

Hans Scharoun, Villa Schminke, 1930–1933, Löbau, Germany
Scharoun's designs could not have been further removed from Modernist contemporary buildings such as Mies van der Rohe's Villa Tugendhat and Le Corbusier's Villa Savoye. Scharoun's design consisted of irregularly shaped slabs which curved out towards the exterior garden, as advocated by Mendelsohn. The villa has receding glass curtain walls which allow the maximum interface between the interior and the exterior environments. The villa is rather like the prow of a ship, the main body of which faced in the direction of the owner's factory.

NEW ENGLISH GARDENS

Over the years garden design had been classified into what appeared to be rigidly set categories: Italian, French and English gardens, with a few exotic variations, such as Islamic, Andalucían, Japanese and Chinese gardens. However, in the early 20th century, a new way of conceiving the historical relationship between gardens and the surrounding landscape, and between domestic gardens and the surrounding woodland, began to develop. Gardens started to be planned and appreciated as organisms that transformed with the changing seasons; there was a far greater use of flowers and colours. Thus artistic gardens were created.

Gertrude Jekyll (1843–1932), an Englishwoman from the upper echelons of society, was the creative spirit responsible for this development. Jekyll had been working with the landscape artist/architect, Edwin Lutyens (1869–1944), who was the mastermind of New Delhi and who had designed over a hundred gardens since the early 20th century — all of which had been planned with this new philosophy in mind. Jekyll published her ideas widely, especially her concepts regarding colour schemes for flower gardens. She created handbooks — with great artistic sensitivity and botanical knowledge — for choosing flowers and bushes that would produce different, changing chromatic effects throughout the year. Gardens were influenced by Late Eclecticism and Art Nouveau decoration and were thus designed with flowerbeds arranged in various ways, densely packed with flowers. A section of these gardens was allowed to grow wild, to create an area where herbs and flowers could grow rampant and untended. Meanwhile, alongside these so-called 'artistic gardens' William Robinson (1838–1935) was working on the theory of 'wild gardens' which, if planned with the same care, diversity and understanding, could grow freely, producing an illusion of natural spontaneity. Both types of garden were tremendously successful and, from 1930 onwards, formed the blueprint for a great many gardens.

below
Gertrude Jekyll, view of the garden at Manor House, 1908, Upton Grey, England
The gardens at Manor House was one of the earliest 'artistic gardens'; the flowerbeds are devoid of trees, containing rather an assortment of flowers and bushes, both indigenous and exotic, planted alongside each other in order to produce striking chromatic effects that transformed with the changing seasons. These gardens were to allow for contemplation, with islands of flowers planted within the verdant landscape.

opposite page
William Robinson, Garden at Ninfa, 1922, Latina
As the planting was left in its natural state, 'wild gardens' were the antithesis of 'artistic gardens'. However, both types of garden were derived from the same sophisticated botanical knowledge and both descended culturally from Eclecticism.

SCANDINAVIA

Modern architecture began to take root in Scandinavia after 1930. Erik Gunnar Asplund (1885–1940), who was working in Sweden, spent some time researching classical and traditional forms before refining his style, designing Rationalist works such as the Bredenberg Department Store in Stockholm (1933–1935) as well as the extension to the City Hall in Gothenburg (1934–1937). The harmonious proportions of the façade relate well to the adjacent 19th century building; it has an internal covered courtyard with galleries leading to office spaces and timber-panelled walls. The city hall is reminiscent of Frank Lloyd Wright's Larkin and Johnsons Wax buildings, a blend of the intended 'homeliness' of the public spaces and the need for enclosed spaces as dictated by the cold Scandinavian climate. Asplund's major projects were inspired by a rationally simplified knowledge of Classicism. His library in Stockholm (1920–1928) consists of a vertical cylinder set in the centre of a three-storey square block. The building has the stature of an Illuminist design, inspired by Étienne-Louis Boullée (after an early design borrowed from Claude Nicolas Ledoux), a precursor of Post-Modernism. The crematorium at Stockholm's Woodland Cemetery (1940) has an orthogonal porticoed structure with a central impluvium, devoid of any ornamentation. The ensemble of buildings responds to nature, set within an expanse of grassland, one arrives at the crematorium along a white pathway — metaphoric of the path of hope or redemption — against the backdrop of the woodlands. The crematorium is a kind of modern interpretation of the Parthenon.

The leading exponent of Rationalism in Denmark was the world-renowned architect and designer, Arne Jacobsen (1902–1971). Jacobsen designed the Bellavista Residential Development near Copenhagen in 1935; the complex consists of staggered, flat-roofed white volumes, all of which face out to sea. He also designed the Århus City Hall (1941), which consists of several offset volumes with a tall tower, a carefully balanced composition, recalling works by Dudok.

Erik Gunnar Asplund, external view of the Stockholm Library, 1920–1928, Stockholm
A Classical building, modelled on Illuminist works, it is a precursor of Post-Modernism. The library consists of an orthogonal volume containing offices, with a protruding cylinder which houses the reading room. The two contrasting forms were designed to counter balance one another and have been carefully combined using harmonious proportions.

THE LITURGICAL MOVEMENT IN GERMANY

The Liturgical Movement was established in Germany during the 1920s; it was geared to analysing and defining the design of the new churches in order to enable the congregation to have a more direct role in the liturgy. The theologian of the movement was Romano Guardini who was born in Verona, but resident in Germany at that time. (Guardini was also a source of inspiration for Mies van der Rohe after 1930). He published *The Spirit of Liturgy* in 1918, immediately after the First World War had ended. The members of the movement met in the Knights' Hall at Rothenfels Castle, where the new liturgical plan layouts were discussed. The architects who subscribed to the movement were Rudolf Schwarz, who was the leader, Emil Steffann, Hermann Baur and Fritz Metzger. The latter built several churches in Switzerland and Germany in collaboration with Dominikus Böhm. The aim of the Liturgical Movement was to try and reduce the distance between the ministers and the congregation and between the faithful and the altar.

Rudolf Schwarz (1897–1961), an adherent of the Rationalist and Bauhaus movements, planned simple churches composed of elementary volumes, for example the Corpus Christi Church in Aachen (1930). Dominikus Böhm (1880–1955) designed churches with fluid, often symbolic forms, such as the church of St Engelbert in Cologne (1930–1932). The church is built to a circular plan, it is composed of parabolic brick arches that support a cupola, according to the design he executed in 1922 together with Martin Weber. The building was appropriately named 'Circumstantes', after the circular, 'surrounding' layout for the congregation. St Engelbert was the movement's first concrete manifesto.

The architect, Emil Steffann (1899–1968) adhered to the same tenets, building very simple buildings, known as 'stable churches' in memory of the early 13th century Franciscan churches. These architects also planned the liturgical remodelling of a great many churches in Germany and remained active right up to the 1950s.

below, left
Dominikus Böhm, exterior of the Church of St Engelbert, 1930–1932, Cologne, Germany
Böhm designed a circular layout for the church, enabling the congregation to be gathered around the altar. The form of the church is accentuated by the high, unusual parabolic vaults. The building is extremely original; it is Neo-Gothic in spirit with references to medieval architecture. The dynamic thrust of the volumes and the lighting effects inside the building create a highly suggestive atmosphere.

below, right
Rudolf Schwarz, exterior of the church of Corpus Christi, 1930, Aachen, Germany
Schwarz successfully responded to the aims of the movement with this church in Aachen. The church has a smaller presbytery, which faces the longitudinally-arranged congregation. Schwarz deliberately designed the architecture to be clear and simple.

ARCHITECTURAL ENGINEERING

Every building has a structural frame that may not be obvious at first glance. There are, however designs that can be functionally pared down to their structure, such as bridges and hangars. Several engineers, as well as architects, were involved in designing structures that combined new building techniques with the exploration of meaningful shapes, thereby achieving some fine projects. These engineers mostly worked independently and were not a part of a larger network. Robert Maillart (1872–1940), both an engineer and an entrepreneur, was the most famous engineer of bridges. He built his first stiffened bridge in 1905; he spent a few years in St Petersburg (1915–1918), after which he returned to Switzerland where he built the astounding Chatelard Aqueduct (1924) as well as around a dozen bridges, including the Thurbrücke at Felsegg (1932) which has parallel arches, the bridge at Vessy with X-shaped cross-walls between the concrete slab and the supporting arch and the bridge at Garstatt (1939), where the arch is replaced by a triangular structure. During this period Maillart also designed the boldest of all his bridges at Schwandbach (1933) and the pedestrian crossing over the Toss River (1932). Maillart invented a prototype for each of his structures, in an attempt to develop the most aesthetic possible solutions.

Meanwhile Pier Luigi Nervi (1891–1979) embarked on similar research for different kinds of buildings. Nervi built the football stadium in Florence (1930–1932), with its conspicuous reinforced concrete steps, cantilevered roof and extremely slender spiral staircases projecting from the building like Constructivist sculptures. He also designed roofs for aircraft hangers (1935–1940) constructed from concrete or steel, consisting of diagonally interwoven elements — like basketry — supported by sculptural concrete arches.

The Spanish architect, Eduardo Torroja (1899–1961), was achieving similar results in Spain with buildings like the Zarzuela hippodrome in Madrid. Torroja also invented the concrete shell roof, which was widely used after the Second World War.

Robert Maillart, Bridge, 1933, Schwandbach, Switzerland
The bridge at Schwandbach is one of Maillart's boldest achievements as the road is curved. The bridge is held on a slender concrete slab supported by a delicate arch. The arch is connected by vertical sections which create an extremely refined bridge that blends in sensitively with the alpine scenery around it.

Pier Luigi Nervi, aircraft hangar, 1939, Orbetello, Grosseto
Nervi designed several aircraft hangars for the Italian Air Force. He invented a trellised frame with crossbeams, thus creating slender rhomboids structures that could be easily assembled. Unfortunately almost all his structures were destroyed, with only one at Marsala surviving.

INDEX OF PLACES

PHOTOGRAPHIC CREDITS

Front cover: Ludwig Mies van der Rohe, Barcelona Pavillon (© Hans Engels, Munich, © VG Bild-Kunst, Bonn 2011)

Back cover: Walter Gropius, Bauhaus Dessau (© Hans Engels, Munich, © VG Bild-Kunst, Bonn 2011)

© 2012 Prestel Verlag, Munich, London, New York
© 2012 Mondadori Electa SpA, Milan, for the original edition, all rights reserved

Prestel Verlag, Munich
A member of Verlagsgruppe Random House GmbH

Prestel Verlag
Neumarkter Straße 28
81673 Munich
Tel. +49 (0)89 4136-0
Fax +49 (0)89 4136-2335

Prestel Publishing Ltd.
4 Bloomsbury Place
London WC1A 2QA
Tel. +44 (0)20 7323-5004
Fax +44 (0)20 7636-8004

Prestel Publishing
900 Broadway, Suite 603
New York, NY 10003
Tel. +1 (212) 995-2720
Fax +1 (212) 995-2733

www.prestel.com

Library of Congress Control Number is available;
British Library Cataloguing-in-Publication Data:
a catalogue record for this book is available from the British Library; Deutsche Nationalbibliothek holds a record of this publication in die Deutsche Nationalbibliografie; detailed bibliographical data can be found under http://dnb.d-nb.de

Prestel books are available worldwide. Please contact your nearest bookseller or one of the above addresses for information concerning your local distributor.

Editorial direction: Stella Sämann
Translation: Bridget Mason
Copyediting: Anna Roos, Bern
Cover: Sofarobotnik, Augsburg & Munich
Production: Astrid Wedemeyer
Typesetting: Wolfram Söll, Munich
Printing and Binding: Mondadori Printing, Verona

Printed in Italy

ISBN 978-3-7913-4641-0

FSC
www.fsc.org
MIX
Paper from
responsible sources
FSC® C018290

Verlagsgruppe Random House FSC-DEU-0100
The FSC-certified paper Respecta Satin has been supplied by Burgo cartiere (Italy).